W9-AXK-010

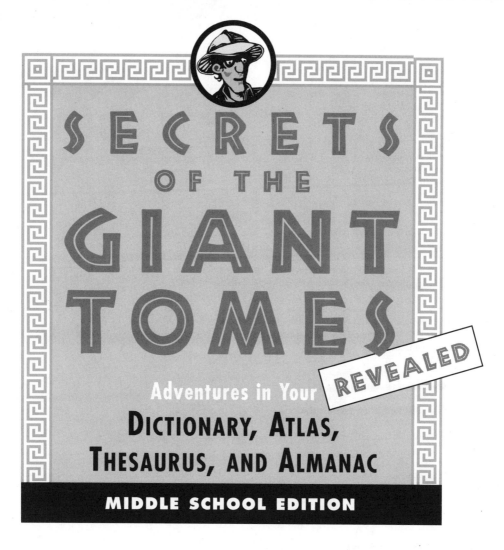

SECRETS OF THE GIANT TOMES REVEALED

Adventures in Your

DICTIONARY, ATLAS, THESAURUS, AND ALMANAC

MIDDLE SCHOOL EDITION

BY CHRIS KENSLER

A Paper Airplane Project

Simon & Schuster
New York • London • Sydney • Singapore • Toronto

Kaplan Publishing
Published by Simon & Schuster, Inc.
1230 Avenue of the Americas
New York, NY 10020

Copyright © 2002 by Chris Kensler and Heather Kern

All rights reserved. No part of this book may be reproduced or transmitted in any form or by any means, electronic or mechanical, including photocopying, recording, or by any information storage and retrieval system, without the written permission of the Publisher, except where permitted by law.

For bulk sales to schools, colleges, and universities, please contact: Order Department, Simon & Schuster, 100 Front Street, Riverside, NJ 08075. Phone: 1-800-223-2336. Fax: 1-800-943-9831.

Kaplan® is a registered trademark of Kaplan, Inc.

Cover Design: Cheung Tai
Cover Illustration: Jeff Foster
Interior Page Design and Production: Heather Kern

Manufactured in the United States of America

October 2002

10 9 8 7 6 5 4 3 2 1

Library of Congress Cataloging-in-Publication Data is available.

ISBN 0-7432-3524-X

ABOUT THE AUTHOR

Chris Kensler majored in English at Indiana University. He has written over a dozen books, covered a presidential campaign for a national news organization, and edited an arts and culture magazine. He is co-founder of the book packager Paper Airplane Projects with his partner, Heather Kern.

ACKNOWLEDGMENTS

The author would like to thank Maureen McMahon for her help shaping and editing the manuscript and Lori DeGeorge for proofreading the book.

TABLE OF CONTENTS

TENNESSEE TOLEDO AND HIS

DESERT OF DANGER

Tennessee Toledo pulled his sports utility vehicle to the side of the desert road and went for a stroll under the stars, searching the sky for constellations. The beginner treasure hunter was taking the night off in his search for the tomb of Mia Pharaoh, the legendary Queen of Egypt.

"I see Cassiopeia and Orion," he said, looking up. "There's the Little Dipper and the Bi-"

Suddenly, the sand beneath his feet shifted, and Tennessee went tumbling into a giant crevasse formed by a recent earthquake. His water bottle flew one way, his walking stick the other. He careened down the ravine, deeper and deeper into the earth.

"Woe is me!" he yelled. "This is surely my desert of disaster!"

Tennessee hit his head on a rock and went out like a light. He awoke flat on his back. He opened his eyes, but all around him was as black as a moonless night.

Tennessee lifted himself to a sitting position, holding his throbbing skull. He thought he heard footsteps. He tensed. "Is anyone there?" he called.

The sound of his echoing voice was his only reply. Tennessee was in a room or a cave or something—he couldn't tell in the total blackness. He got up and felt around carefully, taking baby steps, arms outstretched.

"Hello?" he tried again. "Anyone?"

A woman's voice responded!

"Big Phrank, is that you?" she said. "How did you get into the library without the key? Let me switch on the light."

Suddenly the room was awash in the brightest light Tennessee had ever seen, reflecting off walls made of solid gold. He protected his eyes with his hands and squinted at the figure before him. As his pupils narrowed, he could not believe his eyes. It was Mia Pharaoh! The legendary Queen of Egypt!

"You are not Phrank the Large!" the mummified queen screamed. "You are an intruder!"

"No no!" Tennessee protested. "I fell through a hole in the desert, and—"

"Big Phrank! Little Woodrow! Purrty Kat!" the queen called out, and before Tennessee could finish his explanation, Mia Pharaoh was joined by three angry mummies—a large man, a small man, and a small animal.

"Get the intruder!" she ordered.

The mummies chased Tennessee around the golden library. Books and scrolls flew everywhere, old tables were overturned, chairs were smashed.

"If you'll just let me explain!" Tennessee yelled back over his shoulder, but no one was listening. Finally, the mummies cornered him on top of a twenty-foot book-

case. Tennessee was dead meat.

TRAPPED BY MUMMIES!

"Can we just leave him up there to die?" asked the shorter mummy. "I mean, he's good and trapped!"

"Stop your sniveling, Woodrow," the queen barked. "Go up there and get him and bring him to me."

"Do what the lady says, shorty," said Phrank the Large.

"Meow!" hissed the mummified cat.

"Oh geez, alright, just a minute, let me tie up my mummy wrap nice and tight here," Woodrow the Small stalled.

"If you won't crawl up, I'll heave you up," Phrank the Large said, and, taking

Woodrow the Small by his mummy wrap, tossed the puny mummy to the top of the bookcase.

"Gotcha!" said Woodrow, grabbing Tennessee around his belly. "Don't even think of escaping now you, you . . . library wrecker!"

Little Woodrow and Tennessee climbed down the bookcase. Woodrow gave Tennessee a little shove toward the queen, then ran back to hide behind Phrank the Large and the mummified animal.

"You have one minute to explain yourself, intruder," said Mia Pharaoh. "Then you shall die a gruesome death at the claws of Purrty Kat!"

"Meow!" hissed the cat mummy.

"First, let me say it's an honor to make your acquaintance, Ms. Pharaoh," Tennessee stammered. "My name is Tennessee Toledo. I am a beginner treasure hunter. I was taking a walk in the desert when I fell into your legendary tomb. Tell me, is the legend true? Are there really two priceless 100-foot statues of your two husbands, Phrank the Large and Woodrow the Small, in this tomb?"

"Maybe there are,

and maybe there are not," replied the queen. "You shall never know. Purrty, sharpen your claws!"

"No, wait!" Tennessee stalled. "I've made a huge mess of your library. Please just let me straighten up before Purrty shreds me to bits." Tennessee began putting books back onto their shelves and re-rolling scrolls. Then he noticed something.

"Do you realize your reference books are really outdated?" he asked.

"Waddya mean?" Phrank the Large interrupted. "Whenever I get sick of practicing scales on my gourd flute, I update the atlas and almanac with whatever places and facts come into my head. Those tomes are aces!"

"Our dictionary and thesaurus are in great shape, too," Woodrow the Small added. "For instance, I made up a new word yesterday: *behmehlep.* It means 'short but sweet.' I put it in the dictionary under 'B' and I put it in the thesaurus as a synonym for *woodrowlike.*"

"Phrank, are you saying that my reference

books are full of information that you and Woodrow the Small just . . . make up?" the startled queen demanded.

"That's right, doll," said Phrank. "There's no need to worry about the tomes with me and Woodrow on the case."

"I married idiots!" screamed Mia Pharaoh. "This is your lucky day, intruder."

MIA PHARAOH'S GAUNTLET OF GIANT TOMES

"I will spare you the claws of Purrty Kat if you update my ruined tomes," she offered. "To keep things interesting, I will make a game out of it. I will put each of my giant tomes—my WORLD ALMANAC, WORLD ATLAS, DICTIONARY, and THESAURUS—in a separate chamber of my vast library."

"I like it, I like it!" yelled the excitable Woodrow. "It's like a maze or something!"

"Silence!" ordered the queen. "Only by completely updating one tome will you be granted access to the next room. And only by updating all four of the reference books can you make it through my . . . well, what shall we call it?"

"How about your *Gauntlet of Giant Tomes*!" Woodrow offered.

"That is why I married you Woodrow. You are so clever!" complimented the queen.

"It sounds like quite a challenge," said Tennessee. "I'll do it on one condition. If I make it through your Gauntlet of Giant Tomes, I win those statues."

"Why I oughta pop you one!" said Big Phrank, raising his fist.

"Deal!" the queen agreed. "In each chamber, you can earn one word of a four-word password that will reveal the price-less statues of Phrank the Large and Woodrow the Small. If you learn the pass-word, you earn the statues!"

"Our priceless statues made of gold and jewels!?!" the two mummies cried.

"Yes, your statues!" repeated the queen. "You two have disappointed me greatly. If Tennessee res-cues my tomes, losing your precious statues is the price you will pay! Now go and prepare the tome chambers!"

"I'll get you for this, treasure boy," Phrank threatened, brushing past Tennessee and jabbing him in the side with his gourd flute.

"We will see you in the first chamber,"

PALMSPRING 7000

Tennessee's PDA has a special feature. You can write notes to Tennessee on this book's special HyperTrans paper, and Tennessee will get your messages on his handheld PalmSpring 7000!

said the queen. "It is the first door on your right. Come on, Purrty Kat."

With the mummies gone, Tennessee took a deep breath. He had averted being scratched to death by a mummified cat, but now he really had his work cut out for him. Tennessee was a pretty bright explorer, but it wasn't like he had the dictionary, atlas, thesaurus, and almanac *memorized*.

Tennessee was worried. He didn't know how he could possibly update Mia Pharaoh's big, outdated reference books.

But wait!

Just before he set off for Egypt, Tennessee's inventor friend Leonard had given him a homemade handheld computer. Leonard called it his PalmSpring 7000 Personal Digital Assistant. Leonard's PalmSpring PDA has a special feature. People can write notes to Tennessee on HyperTrans paper, and Tennessee can receive the notes on his PalmSpring! Maybe Tennessee could get the answers to Mia Pharaoh's questions on his PalmSpring 7000!

"This may work!" Tennessee exclaimed. "If I can type out questions about Mia Pharaoh's reference books and get the answers back from the outside world, I may just make it through her Gauntlet of Giant Tomes!"

THIS IS WHERE YOU COME IN

Tennessee begs the readers of this book to give him the information he needs to survive the Gauntlet of the Giant Tomes. All you need to do is use your modern-day WORLD ATLAS, THESAURUS, WORLD ALMANAC and DICTIONARY.

Secrets of the Giant Tomes Revealed is printed on Leonard's special HyperTrans paper! When you write your answers in the book, the answers are automatically transmitted to Tennessee's PalmSpring 7000. (Don't believe it? Check out the antenna on the back cover.)

If you and the other people who have this book complete all of the activities, Tennessee can get all of the information he needs to update the queen's ancient tomes. With your help, Tennessee can make it through Mia Pharaoh's Gauntlet of Giant Tomes, win the priceless statues, and gain his freedom. Otherwise, he's cat food.

HOW TO USE THIS BOOK

Tennessee Toledo has to make it through four chambers of Mia Pharaoh's tomb so he can gain his freedom. In each chamber, you need to do a bunch of fun **Inter-Activities** involving a reference book in order to save Tennessee from the mummies.

For each of these activities, you need a standard, adult version (NOT a kid version) of one of these reference books:

World Almanac   Dictionary
World Atlas   Thesaurus

Most activities also have a short **Tome Test** question that leads you into a deeper exploration of your reference book. Other activities have **Tome Tips** to help you learn more about your reference book.

So you need these reference books by your side to do the Inter-Activities and Tome Tests. Once you complete all of the activities in one chamber, you will be given a final challenge called **Mia Pharaoh's Dangerous Puzzle of Pain**. It tests all of the skills you learned.

The Dangerous Puzzle of Pain reveals the **Extra Dangerous Password**. If you collect the passwords from all four chambers, you can help Tennessee get his treasure and escape.

Let's recap. In each chamber you need to:

1 Do the Inter-Activities

2 Do the Tome Tests and Read the Tome Tips

3 Complete the Dangerous Puzzle of Pain

4 Collect the Extra Dangerous Password

OKAY, BUT WHAT'S IN IT FOR YOU?

These activities will help you get really good at finding information in a dictionary, almanac, thesaurus, and atlas. Knowing how to use these books will help you with homework, papers, and tests.

MAKE YOUR PARENT OR TEACHER READ THIS PART

The Inter-Activities in this book are designed for your student to complete on her own, or with someone's help. If she works on her own, she will probably need your help once in a while, either with a challenging activity or to check her answers.

You can use any good, recently published reference book to help Tennessee Toledo, but some reference books work a little better than others. Tennessee recommends the following reference books.

WORLD ALMANAC

Use a world almanac published in the last year or two. It is very important to use an up-to-date almanac. You don't want an almanac from 1981 because everything that has happened since 1981 won't be in there. Also, make sure your world almanac has the following kinds of information:

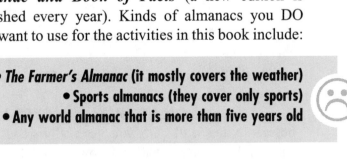

- **Population facts and statistics (world and U.S.)**
- **United States facts and statistics (U.S. presidents, elections, state facts, etc.)**
- **Economic statistics (consumer information, trade statistics, employment statistics, etc.)**
- **History (world history, U.S. history, year in review, etc.)**
- **Sports and awards (Olympics, pro sports, Nobel Prize winners, etc.)**

Tennessee recommends the most recent *World Almanac and Book of Facts* (a new edition is published every year). Kinds of almanacs you DO NOT want to use for the activities in this book include:

- ***The Farmer's Almanac* (it mostly covers the weather)**
- **Sports almanacs (they cover only sports)**
- **Any world almanac that is more than five years old**

None of these will give you the information Tennessee needs to survive the Gauntlet of Giant Tomes.

Note: The answers to the activities in this book come from the *World Almanac and Book of Facts*.

WORLD ATLAS

Use a full-color world atlas for the Inter-Activities in this book.
The atlas should have:

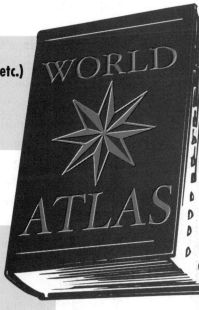

- Maps of all the continents (North America, Asia, etc.)
- Maps of major regions and countries on the continents (U.S., Europe, etc.)
- Maps with physical features (mountains, deserts, lakes, etc.)
- Maps with political features (countries, states, cities, etc.)
- Maps with man-made structures (roads, trains, cities, etc.)

Tennessee recommends *Goode's World Atlas: 20th Edition*
and the *Oxford Atlas of the World*. Kinds of atlases you
DO NOT want to use for this book include:

- Road atlases (they just give driving directions)
- Any world atlas more than ten years old (country and city
  names and boundaries change, new roads and bridges are built, etc.)

Note: The answers to the activities in this book come from
Goode's World Atlas: 20th Edition (Rand McNally).

DICTIONARY

Use a hardcover version of a college dictionary. Don't worry—just because it's a college edition doesn't mean you have to be in college to use it! College dictionaries just have more information about words. Pick a dictionary that includes:

- **Pronunciation information**
- **Etymologies (information about word origins)**
- **Multiple definitions**

Tennessee recommends ***Merriam Webster's Collegiate Dictionary: 10th Edition*** and ***American Heritage Dictionary: Second College Edition***. The kinds of dictionaries you DO NOT want to use for this book include:

- **Most pocket/paperback dictionaries (they usually don't have as much information in them because they are smaller)**
- **Biographical dictionaries (they're good for information about people, but not for words)**

Note: The answers to the activities in this book come from *Merriam Webster's Collegiate Dictionary: 10th Edition*.

College Edition

Dictionary

THESAURUS

Any good English language thesaurus will help you with the activities in this book. Tennessee recommends a thesaurus that has:

- An index of word categories (a list of the subjects used to organize the words)
- An index of words

Tennessee recommends ***Roget's International Thesaurus: 5th Edition***. Kinds of thesauri you DO NOT want to use for this book include:

- A really old thesaurus (common synonyms change as the English language changes over the years)

Note: The answers to the activities in this book were found using *Roget's International Thesaurus: Sixth Edition*.

THESAURUS

More than
250,000
WORDS

IF YOU DON'T READ THIS YOU'LL BE SORRY!
You can do the Inter-Activities in this book with ANY reference book described on these pages. BUT—and this is a very big BUT—if you use reference books that are different from the ones we recommend, your answers to the Inter-Activities will not match up exactly with the answers in the back of this book. THIS IS NOT A BIG DEAL. The important thing is for you to get to know your reference books, no matter what brand they are. But if you want to be able to check your answers, by all means, use the books we recommend.

"W elcome to the first chamber in my Gauntlet of Giant Tomes," says Mia Pharaoh. The room is covered with carpets woven with gold and silver thread. Mia Pharaoh reclines on an overstuffed silk couch and spreads a blanket over her mummy legs. Purrty Kat jumps up and makes herself comfortable while Big Phrank and Little Woodrow stand sullenly in the corner.

In the middle of the room, sitting atop a silver pedestal, is Mia Pharaoh's ancient world almanac.

Tennessee leafs through it. The almanac may be old and outdated but, luckily, it's set up just like a modern-day almanac. It has a table of contents in front, a detailed alphabetical index, and around 1,000 pages of facts and statistics on all sorts of subjects.

Unfortunately, the old almanac is mostly limited to information about ancient Egypt. There are about fifty pages on flute playing; there are only a handful of countries covered in its "Nations of the World" section; and "World History" stops at 2,700 B.C.E.

Tennessee is in serious trouble and desperately needs your help.

Fear the first chamber of
Mia Pharaoh's Gauntlet of Giant Tomes!

Chamber 1

You are Here

Chamber 2

Chamber 3

Chamber 4

EXIT!

FOR STARTERS

Take a few minutes to look through your almanac. What are some of the interesting subjects it covers? Anything you have never heard of?

RESOURCE

World almanac with a table of contents

SKILL

Using a table of contents

ALMANAC SUBJECTS

"Nice tome chamber you have here," Tennessee says, looking around the room as he pages through her dusty book. "Who's your decorator?"

"Calvin Kleinunkamman," Mia Pharaoh replies. "Now tell me intruder, how much have I missed in the last few thousand years?"

"You can call me Tennessee," he replies, studying the giant tome's table of contents. "Well, in your almanac, the world's highest building is 240 hands tall and your almanac's special feature is 'The Year in Clay Pots'. I'd say quite a bit has happened since your time."

"Oh really," says the Egyptian queen, "Like what?"

"Space travel, the internal combustion engine, and a short-in-the-front, long-in-the-back hair style called the mullet," Tennessee jokes. "Anyway, I see I have some work to do getting your almanac up-to-date."

"He talks too much for his own good," Phrank whispers in Mia Pharaoh's ear. "Can I just turn Purrty loose on him now?"

"Not yet," says the queen. "We shall see how he does with this challenge, first."

Inter–Activity

Tennessee needs to organize the subjects listed on the almanac's table of contents page alphabetically, instead of in page-number sequence. This will help him figure out what is missing.

1) On a separate piece of paper, write out all the letters of the alphabet, leaving some space to write beneath each letter.

2) Go through the table of contents in your almanac and copy down each entry under the appropriate letter ("Energy" goes under "E," "Crime" goes under "C," etc.)

3) When you have written them all down, take your alphabetized list and copy it into the three columns on this activity page. (That way it will be transmitted to Tennessee through the special HyperTrans paper used in this book.)

Note: The table of contents has both **categories** and **subcategories**. Subcategories are indented underneath the categories. For this activity, DO NOT list the indented subcategories.

Alphabetical Almanac Contents

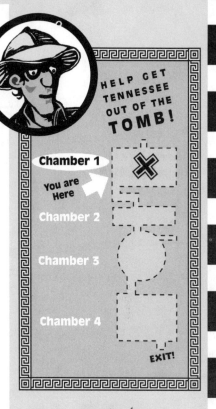

HELP GET TENNESSEE OUT OF THE TOMB!

Chamber 1

You are Here

Chamber 2

Chamber 3

Chamber 4

EXIT!

TOME TEST

Go to the twentieth entry on your alphabetical list. Turn to that entry and write down one fact or statistic you did not know:

RESOURCE

World almanac
with an index

SKILL

Finding information
using a detailed index

USING THE INDEX

t doesn't look like you've missed too much, doll," Phrank says to Mia as they read through Tennessee's new table of contents. "Health, language, sports—we had all that stuff! I think this explorer here is trying to make a fool outta you!"

"I promise I'm not!" Tennessee says. "The table of contents just lists general subjects. There are thousands, maybe millions, of facts and figures missing from your almanac. When we explore the general subjects in detail, you'll really see how much has happened since you guys all died."

"I died first," offers Woodrow the Small. "I was on my way back from the Catapalooza tour, where I opened for Cat Scratch Fever. Ever heard their stuff?"

"I don't think so," says Tennessee.

"They're pretty good. I like their sound. Anyway, I stopped to tie my sandal and was run over by a cart loaded with used kitty litter. The doctors told Mia it wasn't the cart that killed me, it was the stench."

"That's awful," says Tennessee.

"Believe me, I know," says Woodrow. "For my funeral, Mia had her goldsmiths make me a huge, golden pooper scooper. I wear it around my neck sometimes as a reminder."

"Enough with the sob stories," says an impatient Phrank. "I want to see some facts and figures, fast-like!"

Inter–Activity

Tennessee has to update Mia Pharaoh's old almanac with facts about all of the stuff she has missed in the past 5,000 years. Help him by using your index to find facts.

1) Find your almanac's general index (it should be listed in the table of contents).

2) Use your almanac's general index to find ten subjects covered in detail (subjects with a lot of pages devoted to them).

3) Pick a subject to study in more detail.

4) Go to that subject and find five facts you didn't know before.

Ten Subjects Covered in Detail

1)

2)

3)

4)

5)

6)

7)

8)

9)

10)

Five Facts About _____

1.

2.

3.

4.

5.

HELP GET TENNESSEE OUT OF THE **TOMB!**

Chamber 1

You are Here

Chamber 2

Chamber 3

Chamber 4

EXIT!

TOME TEST

What is one subject in your almanac you'd like to see more information about?

_____

Why?

_____

_____

_____

RESOURCE

World almanac with
tables of state statistics

SKILL

Finding information
using tables

READING TABLES

"Yes, Woodrow's passing was a tragedy felt by the entire nation of Egypt," Mia Pharaoh remembers. "For the next few years, we observed a day of mourning on the anniversary of the day he was hit by the litter cart. Then I remarried, and the day of mourning was abolished."

"That's where I come in," Phrank the Large boasts. "I was the only man who could take our great queen's mind off of the little squirt."

"Who are you calling 'squirt'?" Woodrow protests.

"You, my squirty friend," laughs Phrank. "But I don't know what you're sore about. They named a state in Egypt after you—Woodropolis! Not every guy gets a state named after him."

"That's cool," says Tennessee. "I'm named after a state. Tennessee is one of fifty states in the country I came from: the United States of America."

"They should have named my state in Egypt 'Anxiety,'" says Woodrow. "Because that's the state I'm always in. A state of anxiety."

"You can be quite tedious Woodrow," says the queen. "If you do not cheer up I may let Purrty use *you* for a scratching post."

"See why I'm anxious!" yells Little Woodrow, pointing at the queen. "For 5,000 years, this is what I've had to put up with!"

Inter–Activity

Tennessee needs you to find information about the state you live in. Almanacs are full of tables of information about topics like agricultural production and energy consumption, organized by state.

1) Find four different tables of statistics about U.S. states.

2) Write down the title of each table.

3) Write down one statistic about your state from each table.

Your Home State: _____

1. Table Title

_____

Statistic from Your State

_____

_____

2. Table Title

_____

Statistic from Your State

_____

_____

3. Table Title

_____

Statistic from Your State

_____

_____

4. Table Title

_____

Statistic from Your State

_____

_____

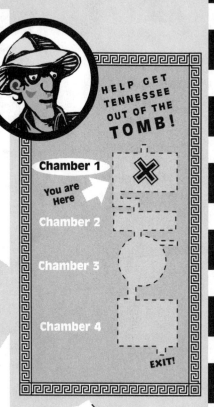

HELP GET TENNESSEE OUT OF THE TOMB!

Chamber 1

You are Here

Chamber 2

Chamber 3

Chamber 4

EXIT!

TOME TIP

There are two good ways to find information about U.S. states.

1) Look up the state name (Tennessee) in the index, then look for the information.

2) Look up the subject (poverty rates) in the index, then look for the specific state.

WORLD

ALMANAC

RESOURCE

World almanac with "Year in Review" section

SKILL

Placing events in chronological order

YEAR IN REVIEW

"If Woodrow the Small's funeral was a big deal, you can imagine what it was like when Phrank the Large kicked the bucket!" boasts Phrank.

"It was the biggest event of that year by far," Mia agrees. "Of course, we had more time to prepare than we did for Woodrow because Phrank's death was not unexpected."

"Says you!" says Phrank. "Big Phrank never backs away from a dare. Never! So when your brother dared me to swim the length of the Nile River, I thought all of Egypt should come out to watch me."

"The whole country knew that Phrank could not do it," Mia Pharaoh explains. "He was incredibly out of shape from staying out late every night playing his gourd flute. So preparations for his funeral were begun immediately after he took the dare."

"Biggest party of the year," Phrank brags. "I just wish I coulda been there. The only thing that happened that year that was bigger than the Chairman of the Gourd dying was the new gold mine they discovered in Az Zaqaziq."

"I bet your little country does not have big events like pharaoh funerals," Mia Pharaoh challenges.

"Sure we do," says Tennessee. "Big things happen every year!"

"Oh yeah? Prove it! I dare ya!" Phrank yells. "I wanna know every big thing that happened in the last year, and we'll see what's bigger, my funeral or your puny country's puny events!"

Inter–Activity

Tennessee needs to provide Phrank with examples of big news events that happened in the last year.

1) There is a timeline drawn on the next page. Write the year you are covering in the space provided.

2) Turn to your almanac's "Year in Review" section. Choose from the year's events the eight things YOU think were the most important. (Most likely, your almanac's "Year in Review" section will cover news from the previous year.)

3) Write them down on the timeline, with their dates, in chronological order.

Your Year

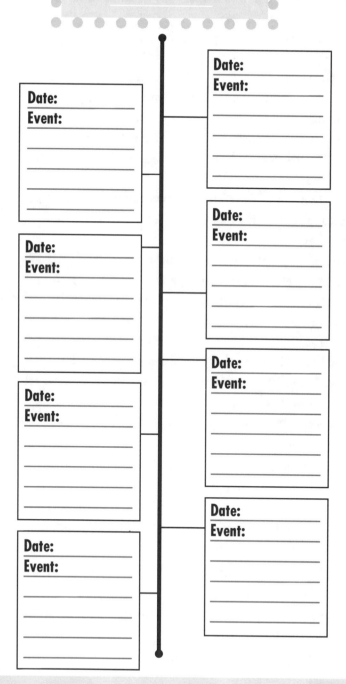

Date: _____
Event: _____
_____
_____
_____

Date: _____
Event: _____
_____
_____
_____

Date: _____
Event: _____
_____
_____
_____

Date: _____
Event: _____
_____
_____
_____

Date: _____
Event: _____
_____
_____
_____

Date: _____
Event: _____
_____
_____
_____

Date: _____
Event: _____
_____
_____
_____

Date: _____
Event: _____
_____
_____
_____

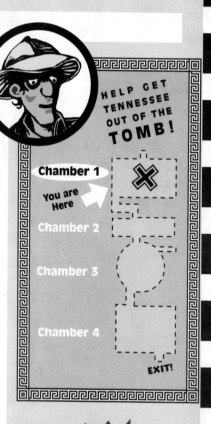

HELP GET TENNESSEE OUT OF THE TOMB!

Chamber 1

You are Here

Chamber 2

Chamber 3

Chamber 4

EXIT!

TOME TEST

Which event in your almanac's "Year in Review" section happened closest to your birthday?

Your Birthday:

_____

Event Date:

_____

Event:

_____
_____
_____

RESOURCE
World almanac with presidential election results

SKILL
Finding and interpreting information in statistical charts

PRESIDENTIAL ELECTIONS

Those are some pretty big things that happened in your country," concedes Phrank the Large.

"Lots bigger than your funeral!" spits Woodrow the Small.

"Says you!" counters Phrank. "Hey, Woodrow, I thought you and me were on the same side. Are you with treasure boy now?"

"With the way you and Mia treat me, maybe I am!" says Woodrow. "Me and treasure boy together make it 2-2, which means I'm finally even!"

"But I get two more votes. One vote, two votes," Phrank smiles, holding up one fist, then the other. "My two extra votes mean you and treasure boy *lose*."

"Actually, in my country, votes really do count," explains Tennessee. "I live in a democracy where we vote for everything—the mayor, student council, even the president of the United States."

"Well, you aren't in the United States, are you treasure boy?" Phrank menaces. "And my two extra votes say YOU LOSE."

"Yes, you lose," Mia Pharaoh agrees, rising from her couch to stand with Phrank. "Like all the losers who came before you! I command you to add to my almanac information about your presidential losers!"

Inter–Activity

Tennessee needs to show Mia Pharaoh examples of really one-sided presidential elections, where the loser got completely smashed by the winner.

1) Find the section in your almanac that contains information about all of the United States's presidential elections.

2) Within this section, find the chart with information about popular and electoral voting results for presidential elections from 1789 to the present.

3) Circle the guy who came in SECOND in each of the presidential elections listed on the next page.

4) Add the political parties and the vote totals for both the loser and the winner.

5) Answer the questions that follow.

Presidential Elections

1936

	Party	Popular Vote Total
Franklin Roosevelt	_____	_____
Alfred Landon	_____	_____

1996

	Party	Popular Vote Total
Bill Clinton	_____	_____
Bob Dole	_____	_____

1984

	Party	Popular Vote Total
Walter Mondale	_____	_____
Ronald Reagan	_____	_____

1956

	Party	Popular Vote Total
Dwight Eisenhower	_____	_____
Adlai Stevenson	_____	_____

1928

	Party	Popular Vote Total
Alfred Smith	_____	_____
Herbert Hoover	_____	_____

How many of these LOSERS were Democrats? _____

Which LOSER lost by the MOST votes? _____

Which WINNER received the FEWEST votes? _____

HELP GET TENNESSEE OUT OF THE TOMB!

Chamber 1

You are Here

Chamber 2

Chamber 3

Chamber 4

EXIT!

TOME TEST

Look at your presidential elections chart.

Who WON in 1964?

_____

Who WON in 1864?

_____

Who LOST in 1972?

_____

Who LOST in 1872?

_____

ECONOMIC STATISTICS

RESOURCE

World almanac with statistics on the U.S. and world economies

SKILL

Finding and comparing information

M eow," meows Purrty Kat.

"What is it?" coos Mia Pharaoh. "Are you hungry? Thirsty? Do you want to use Tennessee or one of my husbands as a scratching post?"

"I think she's pointing at something," says Woodrow the Small.

"Meow," Purrty meows again, and points with a claw to a large diamond on the floor that must have come loose from the diamond studded mural on the room's ceiling.

"Nice rock," says Tennessee, picking up the 4-carat gem. "If I ever ask my girlfriend Georgia to marry me, I'll give her a diamond twice this size."

"Oh really?" says Mia Pharaoh. "Are people in your country all as rich as you are?"

"Actually, I'm not rich at all," Tennessee confesses. "The only rock that I can afford would be a piece of gravel."

"But there are others in the world who *are* really rich, right?" asks the queen. "Fill my almanac with information about riches, intruder. Show me the money!"

Inter–Activity

Tennessee needs to provide Mia Pharaoh with information about the United States economy and facts about the world's other richest countries.

There are a few ways to find the information needed to answer the following questions.

1) Most almanacs have a section on "Economics." Turn to that section first.

2) If your almanac does NOT have this section, or if you are having trouble finding a table or statistic, use your general index to look up the information alphabetically.

3) If you can't find it this way, and the question mentions a country, state, or company name, look that up and see if the information is listed with the place or company.

Almanac Table: U.S. National Income by Industry

1) Which PRIVATE industry had the largest income in 2000?

_____

2) Which PRIVATE industry had the THIRD largest income in 1990?

_____

Almanac Table: Denominations of U.S. Currency

3) Which historical figure is on the:

    $10 bill: _____

    $100 bill: _____

    $1,000 bill: _____

Almanac Table: New Commemorative State Quarters

(Hint: Look in index under *Currency*.)

4) What year did Tennessee get its commemorative state quarter?

_____

5) Which states will get their commemorative quarters in 2008?

_____   _____

_____   _____

_____

Almanac Table: Countries With Highest Gross Domestic Product and Per Capita GDP

6) Which country has the SEVENTH highest GDP?

_____

7) Which country has the highest per capita GDP?

_____

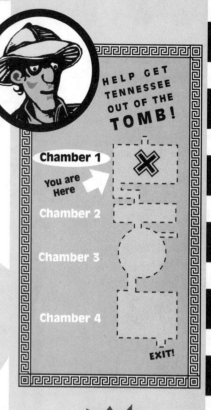

HELP GET TENNESSEE OUT OF THE **TOMB!**

Chamber 1

You are Here

Chamber 2

Chamber 3

Chamber 4

EXIT!

TOME TEST

Find the world gold production table. How much gold was produced in 2000?

_____

Which country produced the most?

_____

RESOURCE
World almanac with
facts about dog breeds

SKILL
Finding and comparing
information

ANNUAL STATS AND FACTS

I am sorry I yelled at you," Mia Pharaoh apologizes. "You see, I have two weaknesses. The first is cats. I love them love them love them, especially Purrty Kat. My second weakness is riches. As you may have noticed, much of my tomb is constructed of gold and precious stones."

"You aren't so different from many Americans," says Tennessee. "I mean, in terms of how you love money."

"Oh really?" says the queen. "Do you love money, too?"

"I'm a treasure hunter, so I guess so," he says. "But I think I like the hunting more than the treasures. Do you know what I mean?"

"No, I do not," replies the steamed queen. "Well, how about cats? Do you like cats?"

"I'm more of a dog person," Tennessee answers.

Phrank the Large and Woodrow the Small dive into a corner and cover their heads. Purrty Kat lets out a yowl like a lioness who just killed her catch.

"Wrong answer, intruder!" Mia Pharaoh seethes.

Inter-Activity

Mia Pharaoh has ordered Tennessee to provide her information on popular dog breeds. He's not sure why, but he has no choice, and he needs your help.

1) Look up your almanac's information on popular dog breeds. You need to find two different tables: the Westminster Kennel Club's winners and the American Kennel Club registrations of popular dog breeds.

2) Answer the following questions about the breeds and winners by comparing the information in both tables.

Note: Keep a bookmark on each table's page because you'll be flipping back and forth.

Dog Show

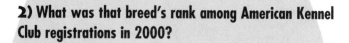

1) What breed of dog won Best-in-show at the Westminster Kennel Club in 2000?

_____

2) What was that breed's rank among American Kennel Club registrations in 2000?

_____

3) Is the breed of 1990 Best-in-show winner Ch. Wendessa Crown Prince one of the Top Ten breeds of 2000?

_____

4) Has the Shih Tzu breed won the Westminster Kennel Club's Best-in-show in the past ten years?

_____

5) Has the Bichon Frises breed won the Westminster Kennel Club's Best-in-show in the past ten years?

_____

6) How many poodles have won the Westminster Kennel Club's Best-in-show from 1991-2000?

_____

7) How many types of terriers won in that timespan?

_____

8) What are the terrier types that won?

_____

_____

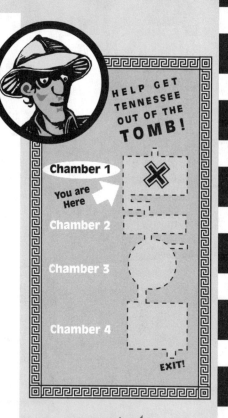

HELP GET TENNESSEE OUT OF THE TOMB!

Chamber 1

You are Here

Chamber 2

Chamber 3

Chamber 4

EXIT!

TOME TEST

Which is your choice for the weirdest dog name among the Westminster Kennel Club's Best-in-show winners?

_____

_____

RESOURCE

World almanac with section on U.S. education system

SKILL

Finding, organizing, and interpreting information

STATISTICAL OVERVIEWS

Ha ha!" cackles the mummified queen. "You have fallen into my trap! By telling me your popular dog breeds, you have exposed those pups to the Curse of the Cat Lover. And that cat lover is me!"

"Not again!" screams Woodrow the Small. "How many cute little dogs have to be turned into goldfish, just because you like cats better?"

"All dogs must be turned into goldfish!" she proclaims. "I had not heard of many of these new breeds, but now that I have, they too will become helpless goldfish flopping on the ground— every cat's favorite meal!"

"Is there anything I can do to stop this from happening?" Tennessee asks, horrified by the evil mummy queen.

"Well, I suppose we could go double or nothing," Mia Pharaoh considers. "If you win, no dogs become goldfish. If I win, you must release the names of ten more dog breeds!"

"Deal," says Tennessee.

"Okay, let me think of a hard one," the queen says. "Here then is your question: Which U.S. state has the best education system, based on the following eight categories?"

Inter–Activity

Tennessee needs to find the following information about state education systems, or a bunch more dogs will be turned into goldfish and be eaten by mean cats.

1) Find each of the following statistics for your state and a neighboring state. Use the contents page and indexes to find the information.

2) Circle the state that has the higher number in each of the categories.

3) Write a one paragraph overview comparing the two states. Which one has higher test scores? Which spends more money on teachers and students? Which state has a better graduation rate?

Note: For all of these statistics, use the MOST RECENT year your almanac has information for.

HELP GET TENNESSEE OUT OF THE TOMB!

Chamber 1
You are Here
Chamber 2
Chamber 3
Chamber 4
EXIT!

EDUCATION STATISTICS

	Your state	Neighbor state
High school graduation rates		
Number of public libraries		
SAT verbal scores		
ACT scores		
Math Achievement Grade 8		
Reading Achievement Grade 8		
Science Achievement Grade 8		
Expenditure per pupil		

Education Overview

_____

_____

_____

_____

_____

_____

_____

_____

_____

TOME TEST

Which of these statistics do you think tells the most about the education systems?

_____

Why?

_____

_____

_____

STATE FACTS

"So which state has the *best* education system?" Queen Mia asks.

"I guess, well, I don't know!" Tennessee admits. "I have given you statistics that point to good and bad things about almost every state's education system!"

"Hooray!" screams Woodrow.

"Aces!" Phrank bellows.

"Hiss," hisses Purrty.

"Drat it all!" mutters Mia. "That was a trick question, and you did not fall for it. Your answer is indeed correct. If you had named a state, I would have been able to put a curse on that state's dogs, too!"

Tennessee breathes a sigh of relief.

"I will find you a goldfish now, Purrty Kat," whispers the annoyed queen and storms out in a huff with her cat.

"Nice job, Tennessee," says Woodrow. "She turned my pooch Thebes into a fish right after we got married."

"And my dog Luxor!" Big Phrank booms. "I miss old Luxor. He was a good dog."

"I miss my dog Joe," Tennessee agrees. "He's waiting for me back in the United States."

"Tell me about the states in your country," says Woodrow. "I mean, are they scary like a bad rash? Or are they sweet, like a fluffy lemon meringue pie?"

Inter–Activity

Tennessee needs to list a bunch of facts comparing three states, including your home state.

1) Go to your almanac's table of contents or general index page.

2) Find the section that gives important facts and statistics on ALL fifty states. Choose two states, including your own.

3) Pick five of the SAME facts or statistics that appear in each state entry. Pick information that might be helpful to a tourist who wants to visit.

Important Facts and Statistics for Tourists

	State 1	State 2
	_____	_____

Tourist Fact 1

_____
_____
_____

➤ _____ _____

Tourist Fact 2

_____
_____
_____

➤ _____ _____

Tourist Fact 3

_____
_____
_____

➤ _____ _____

Tourist Fact 4

_____
_____
_____

➤ _____ _____

Tourist Fact 5

_____
_____
_____

➤ _____ _____

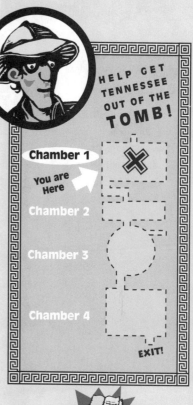

HELP GET TENNESSEE OUT OF THE **TOMB!**

Chamber 1
You are Here
Chamber 2
Chamber 3
Chamber 4
EXIT!

TOME TEST

Write a few sentences about why one state would be the BEST state for a mummy to visit.

_____
_____
_____
_____
_____
_____
_____

RESOURCE
World almanac with
U.S. census figures

SKILL
Finding information
(advanced)

POPULATIONS

Mia Pharaoh returns to the library chamber, but not Purrty Kat.

"I just turned a few of my mummified dogs into goldfish for Purrty's dinner," the queen laughs.

"You know I love you, my queen," Phrank interrupts. "But I cannot stand how you treat dogs."

"Yeah, me too," Woodrow agrees. "What you did to Thebes made me crazy! But we were already married, you were the queen, you had absolute power over me, so I let it go. But now you're just a mummy!"

"Come on, Wood," says Phrank. "Let's go to a tomb where someone appreciates the love of a good pooch."

"You got it, Phrankie!" And with that the miffed mummies were off.

"Well, it looks like it is just you and me, intruder," says the dejected queen. "What did I do that was so bad?"

"You can call me Tennessee," says Tennessee. "And I think you know what you did."

"It is this tomb! Being down here is driving me mad!" explains the queen. "Why can I not travel somewhere where there are people I can talk to, people who share my interest in cats and gold? Where I can meet an older man who can take care of me and my cat?"

"The U.S.A. has a few places with people like that," Tennessee offers.

Inter-Activity

Tennessee needs to give Mia information about the U.S. population. She is concerned mainly with finding places full of older men—the more the better.

There are a couple of good ways to find these statistics.

1) The best way is to turn to your almanac's "U.S. Population" or "U.S. Census" section. All of this information should be there, it just takes a little digging.

2) If you can't find an answer this way, use your almanac's general index to look up page numbers for specific facts and statistics.

U.S. Population Facts and Statistics
(Most recent year available)

1) Total U.S. Population:

_____

2) Total Number of Men in U.S.:

_____

3) Total Number of People 85-older in U.S.:

_____

4) Projected Number of People 85-older in 2050:

_____

5) Most Populous State: _____

    Population: _____

6) State With Highest Population Density: _____

    Population Density: _____

7) Most Populous City: _____

    Population: _____

8) Most Populous County: _____

    Population: _____

9) Metropolitan Area With Most Immigrants: _____

    Number: _____

HELP GET TENNESSEE OUT OF THE **TOMB!**

Chamber 1

You are Here

Chamber 2

Chamber 3

Chamber 4

EXIT!

TOME TEST

Where is the U.S. Center of Population? (That's the geographical point where the U.S. would balance if the number of people on each side of the country was equal.)

Place

_____

Latitude   **Longitude**

NATIONS OF THE WORLD

"Thanks for the tip, intruder," she says. "If I am ever in the U.S.A., I will know just where to go."

"And, of course, there is more to the world than the United States," says Tennessee. "I've been focusing on it because that's where I'm from, and that's what my almanac at home focuses on. But the world has hundreds of other countries to choose from."

"Are there any countries without dogs?" Mia Pharaoh asks.

"What is up with you and the dogs?" counters Tennessee.

"Alright! You have forced it out of me," the queen relents. "As a child I was bitten by a vicious chihuahua, and I have never gotten over it."

"Most dogs are nice," Tennessee explains. "I have a dog named Joe. He's yellow and he has a cold nose. When I give him a biscuit he wags his tail, and he licks my face when I come back from a long trip."

"Oh that is so nice!" Mia melts. "Purrty never does any of that. I am lucky if she lets me pet her!"

"I'll tell you what, why don't I give you a bunch of information about other countries you can visit, and you take your Curse of the Cat Lover off the dog breeds and the dog mummies? Deal?"

"Deal!" the queen agrees.

Inter-Activity

This time, Tennessee needs to pick the categories with which to compare the countries.

1) Turn to your almanac's "Nations of the World" section.

2) Find the entries for the following three countries.

3) Compare the countries using Tennessee's important measures.

	Costa Rica	Mauritius	Mozambique
1) Population			
2) Population Density (per square mile)			
3) Government Type			
4) Chief Crops (top 3)			
5) Number of TVs (per 1,000 pop.)			
6) Daily Newspaper Circulation (per 1,000 pop.)			
7) Life Expectancy Female			
Male			
8) Fish Catch (metric tons)			
9) Literacy			
10) Tourism			

HELP GET TENNESSEE OUT OF THE **TOMB!**

Chamber 1

You are Here

Chamber 2

Chamber 3

Chamber 4

EXIT!

TOME TEST

Tennessee wants Mia to go to the country with the highest fish catch per person so Mia's cat won't need any dogs turned into goldfish.

Which country is best in this category?

Country

_____

Fish catch per person

_____

RESOURCE

World almanac with section on U.S. history

SKILL

Researching U.S. history

U.S. HISTORY

Hey Mia," yells Phrank, re-entering the chamber. "You didn't change those dog mummies into goldfish. I just saw Purrty eating Tender Bittles, not fish. What gives?"

"I lied," admits the shamed queen. "Now that I am a mummy, I have no super powers. I am just an old, shriveled, washed-up has-been. I have not been able to turn dogs into fish since 2,910 B.C.E.! I am such a loser!"

"You sound like me, Mia!" says Woodrow. "I'm always insecure about myself, but you've always been so self-confident."

"It is a mask," says the deflated queen. "My whole life history is a lie!"

"Everybody gets scared," reassures Tennessee. "It's the brave ones who keep going anyway."

"What do you mean?" asks the queen, sniffing back what would have been tears, had she not been a mummy.

"Take United States history, for example," Tennessee explains. "There are lots of times when the U.S.A. didn't know if it was going to prevail or not, like in the Revolutionary War, for example. But we Americans just kept plugging away until, *ta da!*, we became the world's only super power!"

"Are you saying I could still have super powers?" Mia asks.

"Yes, but you could use your super powers for good."

Inter–Activity

Tennessee needs your help writing a timeline of U.S. history for Mia Pharaoh.

Following is a timeline that starts in 1776, with the signing of the Declaration of Independence.

1) Turn to your almanac's "U.S. History" section.

2) Choose four historical occurrences for each century that show courage in the face of adversity. (Try to get four from 1800-1900 and four from 1900-2000.)

3) Write the events down in the boxes provided on your timeline. Fill in the years on the timeline, too.

U.S. History

1776

1800

Year: _____
Event: _____
_____
_____
_____
_____

Year: _____
Event: _____
_____
_____
_____
_____

Year: _____
Event: _____
_____
_____
_____
_____

Year: _____
Event: _____
_____
_____
_____

Year: _____
Event: _____
_____
_____
_____
_____

1900

Year: _____
Event: _____
_____
_____
_____
_____

Year: _____
Event: _____
_____
_____
_____
_____

Year: _____
Event: _____
_____
_____
_____
_____

2000

Today

HELP GET
TENNESSEE
OUT OF THE
TOMB!

Chamber 1

You are Here

Chamber 2

Chamber 3

Chamber 4

EXIT!

TOME TEST

List two things that happened in U.S. history in the year you were born.

Year: _____

1. _____
_____
_____

2. _____
_____
_____

RESOURCE

World almanac
with statistics
on professional sports

SKILL

Finding information

SPORTS

"Tennessee's right," Big Phrank agrees. "When it comes to queens who have stared down adversity, you, Mia Pharaoh, are a champ!"

"Oh Phrank, you are too kind," Mia demurs.

"No no, he's right," Woodrow the Small chimes in. "Remember that time I was getting sand kicked in my face when we were vacationing on the Mediterranean? You had your guards come down and make those Roman bullies stop!"

"That is when I fell in love with you, Woodrow," Mia remembers. "You seemed so . . . cuddly."

"If the gods were to create a woman who was both beautiful and brave in the face of adversity, that woman would be you, Mia Pharaoh!" Big Phrank states.

"Thank you again, Phrank the Large."

"And if there was a sport where the object of the sport was to be brave in the face of adversity, you, Mia Pharaoh, would be that sport's champion!" Phrank continues.

"Yeah yeah," Woody agrees. "They'd give you a trophy with your name on it and everything. Mia Pharaoh: Champion Adversity Facer."

"Add that sport to the sports section of our almanac," Phrank the Large orders Tennessee. "The sport: Facing Adversity. The Champion and Most Valuable Player: Mia Pharaoh!"

Inter–Activity

Tennessee needs to list the champions of a bunch of professional sports.

1) Find the NBA, NFL, NHL and MLB champions for the country's bicentennial in 1976.

2) Find the Most Valuable Player (MVP) in each of these playoff series.

3) Identify the Rookie of the Year for each of the years and sports given.

4) Identify the player who won each of these special awards.

Year: 1976

	Team	Playoff MVP
NBA Champion (basketball)	_____	_____
NFL Super Bowl Champion (football)	_____	_____
NHL Stanley Cup Champion (hockey)	_____	_____
MLB World Series Champion (baseball)	_____	_____

Rookies of the Year

	Player/s
1972 NBA	_____
1998 NFL	_____
1982 NHL	_____
1977 MLB	_____
	American League National League

Award Winners

In order to make this extra challenging, the sports and leagues are not provided. If you don't know the sport that awards a particular prize, try looking up the prize in your index.

	Player/s
1993 Cy Young Award Winners	_____
1990 Art Ross Trophy Winner	_____
1998 John R. Wooden Award Winner	_____
1989 Outland Award Winner	_____
1957 Vezina Trophy Winner	_____

HELP GET TENNESSEE OUT OF THE **TOMB!**

Chamber 1

You are Here

Chamber 2

Chamber 3

Chamber 4

EXIT!

TOME TEST

Which team has won the most Major League Soccer (MLS) championships?

RESOURCE
World almanac listing prize winners

SKILL
Reading and finding information in chronological lists

AWARDS AND PRIZES

What about me?" whines Woodrow. "Sure, you get to feel good about yourself. You're an Egyptian queen! But I've never won anything!"

"You won third prize at the Cairo Nut Shack's Tuesday night stand-up comedy contest," Phrank offers. "That's nothing to sneeze at!"

"Third prize?" Woodrow repeats. "That's not winning—that's coming in third."

"How about the time you beat Purrty Kat in a game of tiddly winks?" Mia tries.

"Yeah, but then she bit my arm off!" Woodrow retorts. "It took me a week to sew it back on!"

"Meow," meows Purrty Kat.

"Well, just because you haven't won anything yet doesn't mean you never will," reassures Tennessee. "There are lots of prizes you can win."

"Oh yeah?" Woodrow counters. "Name them!"

"I have a better idea," Mia states. "Add the winners of the most important modern prizes to my almanac, so Woodrow will know who his competition is."

"But I'm afraid of competition," Woodrow complains. "It makes me break out in hives."

Inter-Activity

Tennessee needs to add lists of award winners to Mia Pharaoh's almanac. Luckily, your almanac has lots of lists of all kinds of award and prize winners.

For this activity, compile the winners of the following awards for the years given. There are two good ways to find the award winners.

1) Look for an "Awards and Prizes" section in your almanac.

2) Look up the awards in your alphabetical index.

Awards, Medals, and Prizes

Award	Year	Winner
Nobel Prize: Literature	1936	
Academy Award: Best Picture	1984	
Caldecott Medal	1992	
Emmy Award: Comedy	1985	
Grammy Award: Album of the Year	1978	
Newberry Medal	1970	
Miss America	1971	
Nobel Prize: Physics	1950	
Spingarn Medal	1991	
Pulitzer Prize: Fiction	1996	
Nobel Prize: Peace	1989	
Tony Award: Musical	2001	
National Book Award: Fiction	1967	
Pulitzer Prize: American Poetry	1982	

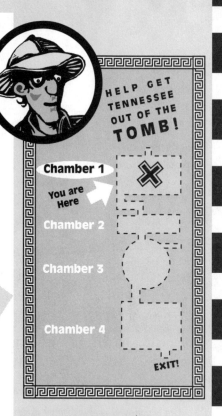

HELP GET TENNESSEE OUT OF THE TOMB!

Chamber 1

You are Here

Chamber 2

Chamber 3

Chamber 4

EXIT!

TOME TEST

What job should you have to win the following medals?

Caldecott Medal

_____

_____

Newberry Medal

_____

_____

RESOURCE
World almanac

SKILL
Using the entire
world almanac

MIA PHARAOH'S DANGEROUS PUZZLE OF PAIN

1

T hat should just about do it," says Mia Pharaoh, paging through all of the new information in her world almanac. "Now it is time to see if you are a big winner, or if you are a big loser."

Tennessee's knees are shaking. Woodrow the Small gives Mia a rolled up scroll. She presents it to Tennessee.

"Here is your first Dangerous Puzzle of Pain!"

Inter—Activity

Complete Mia Pharaoh's Dangerous Puzzle of Pain, which reveals the password needed to get to Chamber 2: The Dictionary.

ACROSS

1 - Greek god who was the father of Zeus
6 - county with the largest population in Maine
7 - the U.S. house of Congress where members serve 6-year terms
8 - 1982 National League MVP (baseball)
9 - U.S. state with the most farms
10 - acronym for the largest professional basketball league
11 - birthplace of President Taft (city)
13 - _____ Trench; seventh deepest point in the oceans
14 - illustrator who won the 1969 Caldecott Medal
15 - home country of 1979 Nobel Prize for Physics winner Abdus Salam
18 - unit of measure used for U.S. meat consumption statistics
19 - the National Basketball Association MVP in 1962

DOWN

1 - Roman ruler in 324 AD
2 - Pacific island that was the site of a major WWII battle in April of 1945 (Hint: check U.S. history)
3 - tenth highest mountain in the U.S., Canada, and Mexico
4 - major candidate who LOST the 1844 presidential election
5 - the first player, alphabetically, in the Pro Football Hall of Fame
8 - the "Magnolia State"
11 - the candidate who won the 1992 presidential election
12 - the U.S. state with the second largest county by population
16 - the U.S. defended this country when it was invaded by Iraq in 1990 (Hint: check U.S. history)
17 - the month in 1855 of the first train crossing of the Mississippi
18 - what symbol goes before the annual percent change in the Consumer Price Index (CPI) between 1996-97, a plus or a minus?

EXTRA DANGEROUS
PASSWORD QUESTION 1

What do the letters in the linked blocks spell?

Password 1

_____

Congratulations! With your help, Tennessee Toledo has made it through the first chamber in Mia Pharaoh's Gauntlet of Giant Tomes.

"My world almanac is perfect," says the queen. "Now I need you to work your magic with my dusty dictionary."

Mia, Phrank, and Woodrow lead Tennessee through a narrow, stone-walled hallway to a second chamber, covered in ancient Egyptian hieroglyphs. On a solid ebony pedestal is her royal dictionary.

It may be old and outdated, but luckily, it's set up just like a modern-day dictionary. It has a bunch of explanatory information in front, followed by about 1,500 pages of definitions. Tennessee thanks his lucky stars that the definitions are in English and not hieroglyphs!

"How did you know English back then?" he asks.

"I did not," Mia Pharaoh says. "But some of the other treasure hunters who have fallen in my tomb did."

DICTIONARY

Beware the second chamber of Mia Pharaoh's Gauntlet of Giant Tomes!

Chamber 1

Chamber 2

You are Here

Chamber 3

Chamber 4

EXIT!

FOR STARTERS

Browse through the explanatory text in the front of your dictionary to learn how the information in the book is presented.

DICTIONARY

DICTIONARY ABBREVIATIONS

Waddya mean, *other treasure hunters*?" Phrank the Large asks. "I don't remember any English-speakin' explorers in here."

"Me neither!" Woodrow the Small agrees. "I thought we all learned English together that year Phrank's priceless statue was receiving satellite TV channels!"

"Bada bing! What a year!" remembers Phrank. "You've got some explainin' to do queenie, and I suggest you do it fast-like."

"Oh Phrank, shut up," Mia dismisses. "I will unleash Purrty on you if you disrespect me one more time."

"Sorry, my queen," Phrank says, shivering at the thought.

"Quite a few explorers have kept me company over the years," she explains. "And many of them have made contributions to my dictionary. I did not want you and Woodrow to get jealous, so whenever a new explorer came along, I dared you to find me some wild geese."

"I told you there were no wild geese in the tomb!" Woodrow fumes at Phrank. "But noooo, Big Phrank *never* backs away from a dare."

"You played us for chumps!" says an enraged Big Phrank. "But we'll have the last laugh! Come on, Wood! Let's plan our revenge."

Phrank and Woodrow storm off, but Mia doesn't care.

"Never mind them," she says to Tennessee. "Now get to work on my tome."

Inter–Activity

Tennessee needs your help figuring out a few of the strange words in Mia Pharaoh's ancient dictionary.

1) Find your dictionary's list of abbreviations and mark the page.

2) Read through the three definitions from Mia's dictionary.

3) Answer the questions that follow, using your dictionary's list of abbreviations.

de·lei·so·nary /di-'lē-zhe-,ner-ē/ *adj.* (1545) **1:** based on or established by adhesion. **2:** sticky (— situation). **3:** unable to slide. **4:** *syn* see ADHESIVE.

quak·a·toot·le /'kwak-ä-,tü-təl/ *n.* [LL *quakatootlus,* fr. L quak-, *chill out*] **1:** cold place. **2:** cold person (as in chilly personali-ty). **3:** *pl* cold fowls. —**quak·a·toot·l·esque** /-tut-l-esk/ *adj.*

stump·sede /stəmp-'sēd/ *vb.* **stumpseded; stumpseding** [ME *stempceden,* fr. MF *stempseder* to chop from, fr. L *stempsedere* to be cut from] **1a:** to cause to be chopped down (— a tree). **b:** to chop away from a larger mass (— a limb). **2:** to render legless (— a frog). **3:** to cause to be immobile with a blow to the clavicle (— an intruder).

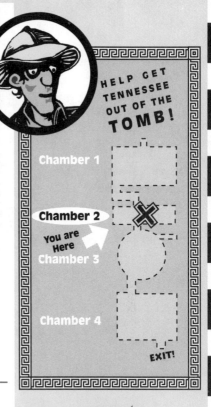

HELP GET
TENNESSEE
OUT OF THE
TOMB!

Chamber 1

Chamber 2

You are
Here
Chamber 3

Chamber 4

EXIT!

1. What part of speech is *deleisonary*?

_____

2. What is the Middle English spelling of *stumpsede*?

_____

3. What language does *stumpseder* come from?

_____

4. Does *quakatootle* come from the Greek language?

_____

5. What is the adjective form of *quakatootle*?

_____

6. What year does *deleisonary* trace to?

_____

7. Circle the stressed syllable of each word:

deleisonary
quakatootle
stumpsede

8. What does the abbreviation in the third definition of *quakatootle* mean?

_____

9. What language does *quakatootlus* come from?

_____

TOME TEST

Tennessee is an *affable* fellow. Answer the following questions about *affable* using your dictionary's definition:

Part of Speech

_____

Latin Form

_____

Noun Form

_____

Synonym

DICTIONARY

SYLLABLES AND PRONUNCIATION

I am sorry you had to see that," says Mia Pharaoh. "There is nothing more uncomfortable than being caught in the middle of another family's squabble."

"Where do you think they went?" Tennessee asks.

"I do not know," says Mia. "Sometimes Phrank likes to cool off in the reflecting pool. Woodrow usually licks his wounds in the embalming room. Anyway, I am not worried. It will give us a chance to get to know each other."

"Great," says Tennessee. "So what's it like being a mummy?"

"It is not so bad, I suppose," she sighs. "I do not have to worry about foreign invaders anymore. I do not have to have my food tasted before I eat it, to avoid being poisoned by family members who want to assume my throne."

"I guess you're right," Tennessee agrees.

"There is one thing I do not like about being a mummy, however," says Mia. "The chapped lips. No matter how much Chap-Stuff I put on them, they are dry as the desert. It really affects my pronunciation of English words. So many consonants!"

Inter–Activity

Tennessee needs to help Mia Pharaoh correctly pronounce her favorite English words.

1) Write out the following English words, using your dictionary's pronunciation guide. DO NOT just go to the definition and copy!

2) Show your new version of the word to someone and ask if he or she can figure out the actual word by pronouncing it just as you have written it.

3) Compare your pronunciation to the version your dictionary provides in the word's definition.

4) Answer the questions that follow.

Word	Pronunciation
beau	
clammy	
desperate	
fake	
family	
hallelujah	
hungry	
love	
marriage	
marvelous	
muscle	
poignant	
shampoo	
virile	

1. Which words DO NOT have a stress on the first syllable?

2. How does your dictionary represent the pronunciation of "-poo" in *shampoo*?

3. How does your dictionary represent the pronunciation of "hun-" in *hungry*?

4. How many syllables are there in the dictionary's pronunciation of the word *family*?

5. How does your dictionary represent the pronunciation of "cla-" in *clammy*?

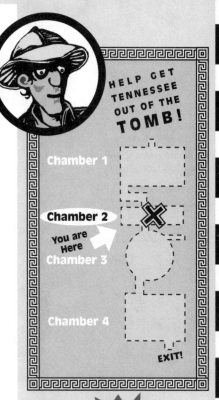

HELP GET TENNESSEE OUT OF THE **TOMB!**

Chamber 1

Chamber 2

You are Here

Chamber 3

Chamber 4

EXIT!

TOME TEST

Write out the pronunciation of your name and Tennessee Toledo's name using your dictionary's pronunciation key.

1.
Name: Tennessee Toledo
Pronunciation:

2.
Name:
Pronunciation:

DICTIONARY

PARTS OF SPEECH

"Oops," says Tennessee. "I dropped your dictionary." He picks it up and a letter pops out.

"It's a love letter from world famous treasure hunter Rowdy Raines!" Tennessee says, surprised. "But he disappeared almost 500 years ago!"

"Rowdy wrote me a letter?" Mia exclaims. "He must have written it before he d-. I mean, before he *left*."

"Left?" Tennessee says. "But he was never found."

"What do you want me to do about it?" Mia asks, annoyed, and grabs the letter. She starts reading, then stops and hands it to Tennessee.

"I do not understand many of Rowdy's words," she says. "Please Tennessee, read me Rowdy's letter, and explain the words."

SKILL
Identifying parts of
speech in dictionary
definitions

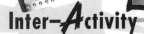

Inter–Activity

Tennessee needs you to clarify some of the words Rowdy Raines uses in his letter to Mia Pharaoh.

1) Look up the **bold-faced** words in Rowdy's love letter in your dictionary (the *italicized* words are for the next activity).

2) Write down (a) how many different parts of speech each word has and (b) what the parts of speech are.

3) Circle the part of speech used in Rowdy's admission of love.

Note: Sometimes a dictionary includes the definitions for multiple parts of speech in a single entry. Other times, a dictionary will have a separate entry for each part of speech's definition. Make sure you use any and all of the entries.

Also: Do NOT include other forms of the word. For example, if the word is *perfect*, do NOT include the parts of speech for *perfectly* and *perfection*. Just list the parts of speech for *perfect*.

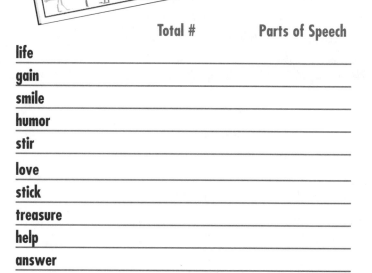

Dearest Mia,

The past *few* days we have spent together in your fancy tomb have been the happiest days in my **life**. Somewhere between your embalming demonstration and your lesson in drying fruit, I started to think of you as more than just a mummy. Yes, I began to think of you as my *friend*. Instead of being nice to you just so I could **gain** my freedom, I found myself liking you for real. Your warm **smile** and dry **humor** won me over.

Then, I felt something else **stir** *deep* within me. When you mentioned your past husbands, Phrank the Large and Woodrow the Small, I grew jealous. Just the thought of you with another mummy made me crazy! Then you gave me a big thank-you smooch. It was then I realized that I **love** my mummy!

Oh Mia, what am I to do? I am a mere mortal who pokes his **stick** in the sand looking for **treasure**, while you are a great, shriveled *queen*, trapped in her tomb. Should I give up the outside world and live by your side here, underground, or try to win my freedom and return to the cruel outside world? Please, **help** me as I search my heart for the **answer**.

Yours forever,

Rowdy

HELP GET TENNESSEE OUT OF THE **TOMB!**

Chamber 1

Chamber 2
You are Here
Chamber 3

Chamber 4

EXIT!

	Total #	Parts of Speech
life		
gain		
smile		
humor		
stir		
love		
stick		
treasure		
help		
answer		

How many different pronunciations are there for the word *live*?

_____

What are they?

_____

_____

_____

_____

DICTIONARY

MULTIPLE MEANINGS

"Oh Rowdy," Mia laments. "If I had known your feelings for me, I never would have let you star-, I mean, *leave*."

"So Rowdy got out?" Tennessee says. "Where was he going next? His disappearance is one of the great unsolved mysteries in treasure hunting."

"I do not remember where he was going next," Mia says, avoiding Tennessee's eyes.

"Because if you do remember, I would be very grateful," Tennessee explains excitedly. "I could follow in his footsteps if I get out of here and-"

"Silence!" yells Mia. "I do not want to talk about it! One more word and Purrty Kat will scratch your eyes out!"

"Bu-" says Tennessee.

"*Sh!*" says Mia.

"Row-" says Tennessee.

"*Sh!*"

"If-"

"*Sh!*"

Tennessee gives up and sits there in silence.

"Good," says Mia. "Now let us get back to the letter. I am having trouble understanding Rowdy. Sometimes he appears to use the same word to mean different things."

Inter–Activity

Tennessee needs to clarify the meaning of some of the words explorer Rowdy Raines used in his heartfelt expression of love for Mia Pharaoh.

1) Write down as many definitions as you can think of for the *italicized* words in Rowdy's love letter.

2) Go to your dictionary and read all of the definitions for the word. Add any definitions you missed

3) Copy down the correct dictionary definition of the word as it is used in his love letter, along with its part of speech.

few
Your definitions:
_____
_____

Dictionary definition as used in letter:
_____
_____

friend
Your definitions:
_____
_____

Dictionary definition as used in letter:
_____
_____

deep
Your definitions:
_____
_____

Dictionary definition as used in letter:
_____
_____

queen
Your definitions:
_____
_____

Dictionary definition as used in letter:
_____
_____

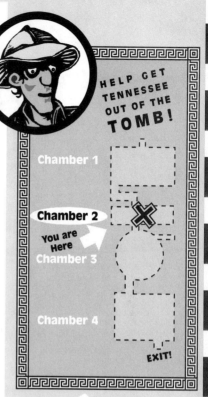

HELP GET TENNESSEE OUT OF THE **TOMB!**

Chamber 1

Chamber 2
You are Here
Chamber 3

Chamber 4

EXIT!

TOME TIP

You'd be surprised how many definitions there are for words you use every day. When you are looking for a word's definition, make sure you read them all to make sure you pick the right one.

DICTIONARY

PREFIXES

D o you know the phrase *It is better to have loved and lost than never to have loved at all?*" Mia asks Tennessee.

"I saw a TV special on the *Lifetime* channel where celebrities talked about what that phrase means to them," Tennessee answers. "Suzanne Somers was the host."

"Suzanne Somers is a liar!" screams Mia, turning away from Tennessee, absentmindedly stroking Purrty Kat. "I would have been happier if I had never met a man."

"What do you mean?" Tennessee asks.

"Rowdy was just the last in a series of failed relationships," she explains. "Before I met Phrank, I thought Woodrow was my one and only. Before I met Woodrow, I was a happy empress, ruling my empire *my way*. And before I was a young empress, I was a girl without a care in the world, happy to play with my cats and read my favorite book series, *The Catsitters Club*."

"Before, before, before," Tennessee repeats. "It's like your life has had a series of prefixes—something that comes before and affects what comes after it."

"Yes!" says Mia. "I guess. What is a prefix again?"

"It's a group of letters that you put before a word to change the meaning of that word," Tennessee explains. "Your dictionary should include a lot of them."

Inter–Activity

Tennessee needs to add information about prefixes, and the words that use them, to Mia Pharaoh's dictionary. He has filled in the first one for you.

1) Find the definitions for the following prefixes in your dictionary.

2) Find one word that uses the prefix.

3) Write a definition of the word that fits with the definition of the prefix. (Some of the words will have LOTS of definitions, but one or two of them should match the prefix's definition best.)

Prefix | Definition

a- _____ on; in; at
dis- _____
inter- _____
mis- _____
post- _____
pre- _____
re- _____
semi- _____
super- _____
un- _____

Word | Definition

abed _____ : in bed

dis _____ : _____

inter _____ : _____

mis _____ : _____

post _____ : _____

pre _____ : _____

re _____ : _____

semi _____ : _____

super _____ : _____

un _____ : _____

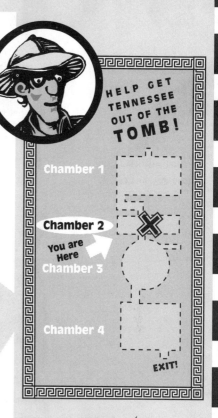

HELP GET
TENNESSEE
OUT OF THE
TOMB!

Chamber 1

Chamber 2

You are
Here
Chamber 3

Chamber 4

EXIT!

TOME TEST

**Use one of the words
you created using
prefixes in a
sentence about
Mia Pharaoh.**

_____
_____
_____
_____
_____

59

DICTIONARY

RESOURCE

English language
dictionary

SKILL

Finding suffixes in the
dictionary and adding
them to words

SUFFIXES

I cannot get my mind off Rowdy!" Mia complains. "The way his floppy hat hung over his left eye at a jaunty angle. The stories he told about his dangerous journeys. The way he called me his *Mama Mia*."

Tennessee is worried. He has to get her mind off the ancient explorer so he can get out of the chamber, and on to those statues!

"You know, my queen," he says to Mia, "we all have relationships that haunt us. For example, before I met my girlfriend Georgia, I went steady with Sarah Michelle Gellar."

"The star of *Buffy the Vampire Slayer*?!" Mia exclaims. "That was my favorite show the year that Phrank's statue picked up satellite TV channels!"

"Yes, that's her," Tennessee admits. "But she couldn't accept that I was a treasure hunter and had to be away for long periods of time. Finally, I knew it just wasn't going to work out, so I wrote Sarah a letter telling her exactly how I felt. It helped me organize my feelings for her, and, eventually, to move on."

"Are you suggesting I do the same thing with Rowdy?" Mia asks.

"Yes," Tennessee replies. "It will help you get over him and continue your afterlife in peace."

Mia Pharaoh writes Rowdy a letter, but many of the words she has used need suffixes added to them for the letter to make sense.

Inter-*A*ctivity

Tennessee needs you
to add suffixes to
some of Mia's words.
Luckily, your dictionary
has the suffix forms
of all these words.

1) Look up the **bold-faced** words in your dictionary.

2) Copy all of the suffix forms of the word that are included in the definition in the space provided.

3) Insert the correct suffix form in Mia Pharaoh's reply to Tennessee.

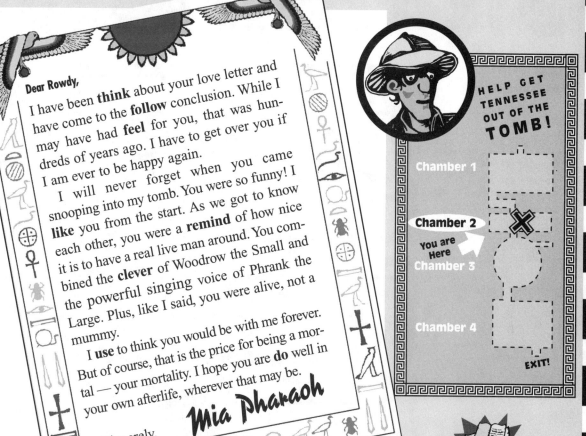

Dear Rowdy,

I have been **think** about your love letter and have come to the **follow** conclusion. While I may have had **feel** for you, that was hundreds of years ago. I have to get over you if I am ever to be happy again.

I will never forget when you came snooping into my tomb. You were so funny! I **like** you from the start. As we got to know each other, you were a **remind** of how nice it is to have a real live man around. You combined the **clever** of Woodrow the Small and the powerful singing voice of Phrank the Large. Plus, like I said, you were alive, not a mummy.

I **use** to think you would be with me forever. But of course, that is the price for being a mortal — your mortality. I hope you are **do** well in your own afterlife, wherever that may be.

Sincerely,

Mia Pharaoh

HELP GET TENNESSEE OUT OF THE TOMB!

Chamber 1

Chamber 2
You are Here
Chamber 3

Chamber 4

EXIT!

TOME TEST

Use two of the suffix forms of these words that were NOT used in Mia's letter to describe her feelings for Rowdy.

Word	Suffix forms (correct form circled)
think	
follow	
feel	
like	
remind	
clever	
use	
do	

DICTIONARY

SPELLING VARIATIONS

"Y ou were right, I feel much better now," says Mia.

"Good," says Tennessee. "I hope you won't mind if I eat in front of you. I'm starving!" Tennessee takes off his backpack and pulls out a stick of delicious turkey jerky. He takes a big bite.

"Is that some kind of sick joke?" Mia asks.

"What do you mean?" Tennessee asks, confused.

"Eating dried flesh in front of a mummy!" she yells. "I have never been so insulted in my life!"

"I'm sorry, it's all I have," he apologizes. "Wait, I think there are some crackers in here somewhere." Tennessee rummages through his backpack. All of his food is gone! Tennessee looks around the room. Purrty Kat is in the corner licking her paws! She has eaten all of Tennessee's food!

"Your cat ate my matzo!" he screams.

"How do you spell that?" she replies.

"There are two ways to spell *matzo*, like it says in your dictionary," Tennessee says, opening her dictionary to *M*.

"Uh oh," he says. "None of the words in your dictionary have secondary spellings."

Inter-Activity

Tennessee needs you to find spelling variants for the words that follow.

1) Look up the following words.

2) Write down the alternate spelling (also known as the *second spelling variant*) for each word.

3) Identify the first spelling as *equal*, *slightly more*, or *much more* common in the "Common Use" column. (Tennessee has filled in "matzo" already.)

Note: When a word has more than one spelling, your dictionary presents it most often in three different ways.

1) By using the word *or* with the two spellings *in alphabetical order,* the dictionary tells you that both spellings are used <u>equally</u>.

ocher *or* **ochre**

2) By using the word *or* with the two spellings *out of alphabetical order,* the dictionary tells you the first spelling is used <u>slightly more</u> often than the second spelling.

plow *or* **plough**

3) By using the word *also* between two spellings, the dictionary tells you the first spelling is used <u>much more</u> frequently than the second spelling.

cancellation *also* **cancelation**

	<u>Alternate Spelling</u>	<u>Common Use</u>
1. matzo	matzoh	equal
2. chili		
3. descendant		
4. eurythmic		
5. karoo		
6. license		
7. pannier		
8. sambar		
9. theater		
10. whizbang		

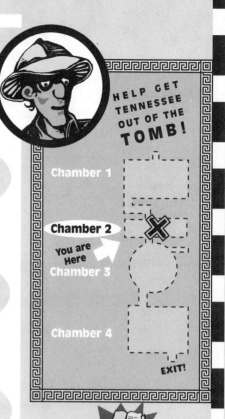

HELP GET TENNESSEE OUT OF THE **TOMB!**

Chamber 1

Chamber 2

You are Here

Chamber 3

Chamber 4

EXIT!

TOME TEST

Some of the words in this activity are rarely used at all. Pick one that you hadn't heard of and write a definition here.

New Word:

DICTIONARY

WORD ORIGINS

Tennessee nibbles on his last stick of jerky as he adds alternate spellings to Mia's dictionary.

"Hey, queen," he says. "You have a bunch of words in here that were coined after Rowdy Raines left. How can this be?"

"I got them from the satellite television channels," she replies.

"What TV show used the word *footlambert?*" he asks.

"Okay, I lied!" Mia admits. "A Japanese explorer dropped by in the 1700s, a French guy came through in the 1800s, and a Russian stumbled on us in 1982. They all helped me before they starved."

Silence.

"I mean, before they *left*," she says meekly.

"They all starved!" Tennessee screams. "Where are they?"

"Right here in this chamber," Mia admits. She opens a door revealing a dozen skeletons sitting around an empty dinner table. Now Tennessee understands.

"Purrty Kat eats everyone's food!" he exclaims.

"It is true," says Mia.

Tennessee only has enough turkey jerky to get him through the day, and after that—nothing! And he's not even out of Chamber 2! Tennessee really has to hurry.

Inter–Activity

Tennessee is suddenly obsessed with food. He also needs your help filling in the etymologies for a bunch of words in Mia Pharaoh's dictionary.

1) Copy down the etymology (history) of the following words from your dictionary.

2) Translate the dictionary's etymology into plain English using (a) your dictionary's list of abbreviations and (b) your dictionary's explanatory section on how the etymology entries work. (Tennessee has done the first one for you.)

Note: If you've never explored word origins before, check out the section on etymology in your dictionary's "Explanatory Notes."

cake *n.*

Dictionary etymology: [ME, fr. ON kaka; akin to OHG kuocho cake]

Translation: Cake comes from Middle English, which took the word from the Old Norse kaka, a word like the Old High German word kuocho, which means "cake."

candy *n.*

Dictionary etymology:

Translation:

chicken *n.*

Dictionary etymology:

Translation:

fish *n.*

Dictionary etymology:

Translation:

pasta *n.*

Dictionary etymology:

Translation:

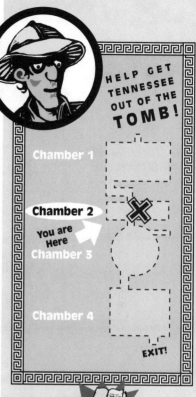

HELP GET TENNESSEE OUT OF THE **TOMB!**

Chamber 1

Chamber 2

You are Here

Chamber 3

Chamber 4

EXIT!

TOME TEST

Some dictionaries also list the date of the first English use of a word. It usually comes right after the etymology. Find those dates for Tennessee's food words.

cake

candy

chicken

fish

pasta

DICTIONARY

RESOURCE

English language
dictionary

SKILL

Finding the Latin roots
for English words

LATIN ROOTS

Tennessee is scared—and hungry! He realizes that this is indeed a life-or-death game, and Mia Pharaoh is a ruthless mummy who loves cats more than people.

"You mean to tell me that you let people starve to death while your mummified cat eats all their food?" Tennessee clarifies.

"I have my reasons," Mia says coldly. "I am a complicated mummy, with many conflicting emotions."

"What kind of conflicting emotions caused you to let these treasure hunters all die down here in your tomb?" Tennessee asks.

"Emotions that only a mummy could understand," she says, petting Purrty Kat. "You don't know me, intruder! You never have and you never will!"

"Maybe if I knew you better I could help you overcome these deadly emotions," Tennessee pleads.

"Fine," she says. "Go ahead and find the roots of my emotions."

"You need to give me hints," he answers. "I can't read minds."

"No," she corrects. "The *Latin roots*. For my *dictionary*, you fool!"

Inter–Activity

Tennessee needs
to get to the roots
of Mia Pharaoh's
mixed emotions.

1) Find the Latin roots of the following words.

2) Find the meanings of the Latin roots, when they are given. (Sometimes, the dictionary won't give a meaning for the root. That usually means the root means what the English root means, or very close to it.)

Note: If you can't find a Latin root for the form of the word, look at the definition for the root form of the word. Find the root of the root. For example, the root form of "elated" is "elate."

The Roots of Mia Pharaoh's Mixed Emotions

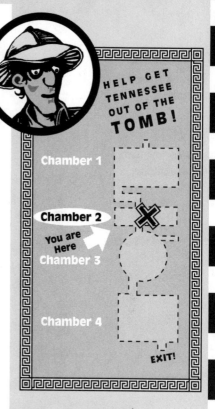

	Latin Root	Meaning
1) confuse	_____	_____
2) distraught	_____	_____
3) dour	_____	_____
4) elate	_____	_____
5) excite	_____	_____
6) incredulous	_____	_____
7) love	_____	_____
8) morose	_____	_____
9) passion	_____	_____
10) sad	_____	_____

HELP GET TENNESSEE OUT OF THE TOMB!

Chamber 1

Chamber 2

You are Here

Chamber 3

Chamber 4

EXIT!

TOME TEST

Of course, not all English words have Latin roots. What languages does the following word come from?

flustered

_____
_____
_____
_____

DICTIONARY

RESOURCE

English language dictionary

SKILL

Using important parts of the dictionary

W "hy did you think Phrank the Large and Woodrow the Small were so scared of Purrty Kat and me?" Mia Pharaoh asks.

"I didn't really think about it, I guess," Tennessee replies.

"It is because I am an unpredictable, ruthless mummy queen who would do anything for my cat!" she exclaims. "They know Purrty comes first, and they are both a distant second."

"Do you think they'll come back?" Tennessee asks.

"Where are they going to go?" Mia laughs. "My tomb does not go on forever. They will be back, begging me for forgiveness."

Tennessee takes his last bite of turkey jerky.

"You had better hurry, Tennessee, if you do not want me to set another place at the table," she cackles.

"What table?" he asks. The queen motions to the table surrounded by treasure-hunter skeletons.

"Oh yeah, that table," says Tennessee, and gets to work on her Dangerous Puzzle of Pain.

Inter–Activity

Complete Mia Pharaoh's Dangerous Puzzle of Pain, which reveals the password needed to get to Chamber 3.

1) Look up the word.

2) Answer the question or questions that follow.

antiheroine

1. What word is this the opposite of?

_____

2. What is the prefix that tells you this?

_____

dog

3. How many parts of speech are there for *dog*?

_____

4. What are they?

_____

hutzpah

5. What is another spelling for *hutzpah*?

_____

6. Is one spelling used more often?

_____

kingdom

7. What school subject is *kingdom*'s LAST definition related to?

_____

muffin

8. Which syllable is stressed in *muffin*?

_____

sister

9. What is the latin root of *sister*?

_____

10. What is its Old Norse origin?

_____

synonymize

11. Give the spellings of *synonymize* with the suffixes –ed and –ing.

_____

love apple

12. What language does *love apple* come from?

_____

13. What is a love apple?

_____

_____

EXTRA DANGEROUS PASSWORD QUESTION 2

What word comes after *phantom* in your dictionary?
Write its plural form here.
Password 2

_____

I do not know how you do it, intruder," Mia admits to Tennessee. "You keep acing my Dangerous Puzzles of Pain!"

"Just lucky, I guess," says Tennessee, buttoning his shirt pocket over his PalmSpring 7000.

"What is that sound?" the queen asks.

"My stomach," groans Tennessee. Luckily, he's stocky and can work off of his fat stores for a while, but for how long?

Mia, Purrty Kat, and Tennessee proceed to the pharaoh's world atlas room. Tennessee leafs through her giant tome. The maps are in bad shape! Tennessee's heart beats faster. How will he ever fill her atlas with maps of the world before he starves to death?

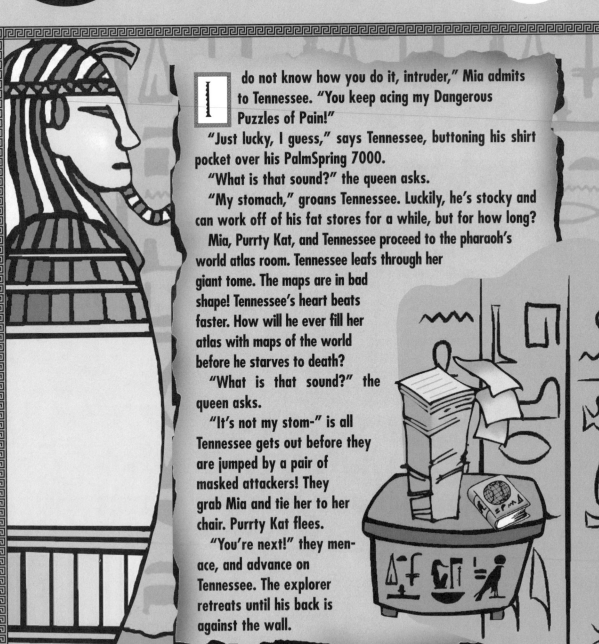

"What is that sound?" the queen asks.

"It's not my stom-" is all Tennessee gets out before they are jumped by a pair of masked attackers! They grab Mia and tie her to her chair. Purrty Kat flees.

"You're next!" they menace, and advance on Tennessee. The explorer retreats until his back is against the wall.

Tremble before the third chamber of
Mia Pharaoh's Gauntlet of Giant Tomes!

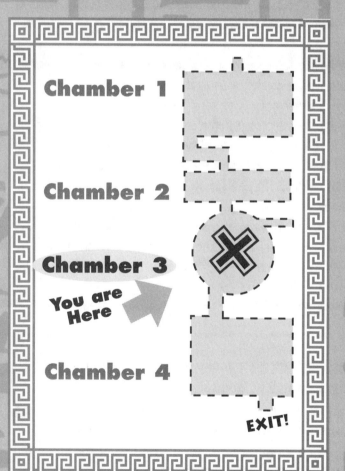

Chamber 1

Chamber 2

Chamber 3

You are Here

Chamber 4

EXIT!

FOR STARTERS

Sit down with your
atlas and go through
it page by page. You
will be amazed at all
of the places in it.

How many of them
do you recognize?

RESOURCE

World atlas with a table of contents and map index

Watch or stopwatch

SKILL

Finding the right map

LOCATING MAPS

W ait a second," says Tennessee. "You guys look familiar."

"Phrank! Woodrow!" yells the seated queen. The mummies remove their masks.

"You welshed on our deal, queenie," says Phrank the Large. "And now we're getting our revenge!"

"What deal?" Tennessee moans.

"We agreed to keep Mia company for the first 5,000 years of her afterlife, and then Phrank and me would be reincarnated," Woodrow explains. "Our 5,000 year anniversary was last week, and she hasn't let us out! If you make it through the gauntlet, Tennessee, we're coming with you!"

"You will never get out of here!" screams Mia.

"Oh yes, we will," says Phrank. "And we've already picked the spots where we want to live. One of your explorer friends left behind a tourism guide for New York City. I want to play my gourd flute across the Hudson River from the city, in Hoboken, New Jersey!"

"And I want to be a stand-up comic in Manhattan!" says Woodrow. "But we don't know how to get there because we don't know how to find the right maps in the queen's world atlas."

Inter–Activity

Tennessee is in a race against time, and so are you. He needs you to time yourself as you find the following places in your atlas using the index and table of contents.

1) Find and mark your atlas's index and table of contents.

2) Set your watch or stopwatch.

3) Time yourself as you look for each of the following places using your table of contents and then your index.

4) Write down how long it took using each resource and which resource was easiest (fastest) to use.

Note: The table of contents is usually a good place to look for big places, like continents (Asia), oceans (Pacific), and regions (Northeastern USA). The index is usually a good place to look for smaller places, like cities (Lima), rivers (Ohio), and mountains (McKinley).

HELP GET TENNESSEE OUT OF THE TOMB!

Chamber 1

Chamber 2

Chamber 3

You are Here

Chamber 4

EXIT!

Place	TOC Time	Index Time
(Circle the fastest resource)		
Africa	_____	_____
St. Louis, Missouri	_____	_____
Russia	_____	_____
Atlantic Ocean	_____	_____
New Zealand	_____	_____
France	_____	_____
Bogota, Colombia	_____	_____
Okefenokee Swamp	_____	_____
Somalia	_____	_____
Aleppo, Syria	_____	_____

TOME TEST

Turn to the map of Somalia and name the largest town or city on its coast on the Indian Ocean.

_____

How do you know it's the largest?

_____

_____

RESOURCE

World atlas with map legend or table of map symbols

SKILL

Reading a map's legend/interpreting a map's symbols

MAP SYMBOLS

"You will never be able to fix my atlas before you starve!" Mia warns. "And even if you do, I will never give you the final password to the statues!"

"Oh yes you will," says Woodrow. "Just wait until you have an itch on your nose that you can't scratch! You'll be telling us all of your secrets!"

"Get going on those maps, treasure boy!" Phrank orders.

Tennessee starts drawing, but all he can think about is food.

"What do all of these symbols mean?" Woodrow asks.

"Lakes, streams, national parks," Tennessee continues. "Cheeseburger restaurants."

"It's a mummy paradise!" Phrank says. "You gotta tell us what all these symbols mean, so we can find a cheeseburger in paradise!"

Inter–Activity

Tennessee needs you to transmit some map symbols to him so he can create a legend for Phrank and Woodrow's map of Mummy's Paradise.

1) Find the page that explains your atlas's map symbols. The symbols page in an atlas is sometimes indentified as its **legend**. Whatever it is called, it typically appears before the maps begin and after any introductory information.

2) Find the following map symbols in your legend.

(over water)	**International Boundary**
(over water)	**Secondary/State Boundary**
	Park
∴	**Ruins**
⊙	**Populated Place: 1,000,000 and over**
○	**Populated Place:** 0 to 25,000
	Major/Principal Roads
	Railroads
✈	**Airports**
	Fresh Water Lake
	Rivers/Streams

3) Place them on the map of the Mummy's Paradise that follows.

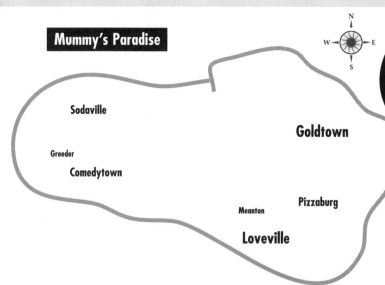

Mummy's Paradise

Sodaville

Greeder

Comedytown

Goldtown

Meanton

Pizzaburg

Loveville

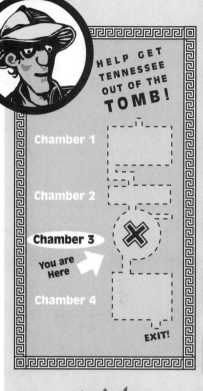

HELP GET TENNESSEE OUT OF THE **TOMB!**

Chamber 1

Chamber 2

Chamber 3

You are Here

Chamber 4

EXIT!

1) Surround paradise with an **international boundary.**

2) Mark Sodaville, Comedytown, and Pizzaburg as **"0 to 25,000 population"** towns.

3) Mark Loveville and Goldtown as **"1,000,000 and over population"** towns.

4) Draw a **secondary boundary** around Sodaville and Goldtown and another one around Comedytown, Pizzaburg, and Loveville, so the map is divided in half.

5) Put a square **park** in the middle of the map, crossing the internal boundary line, but not including any of the towns. Call it *Barefoot Park*.

6) Draw a **railroad** that goes from Sodaville to Goldtown.

7) Put the **ruins** of Greeder and Meanton west of Comedytown and north of Loveville.

8) Draw **major/principal roads** that start at Loveville and go through all of the other towns, and out past Paradise's boundaries.

9) Draw a **river** that passes across Paradise, through Sodaville and Pizzaburg, from Northwest to Southeast. Call it Extra Cheese River.

10) Put an **airport** outside Loveville.

TOME TEST

According to this map, what are two good ways to get from Sodaville to Pizzaburg?

1. _____

_____

_____

2. _____

_____

RESOURCE
World atlas

SKILL
Interpreting
information on a map

DIRECTIONS

Tennessee is light-headed with hunger. He realizes that the map he just drew is nonsense.

"Get your mind off food!" Tennessee says to himself. "You've got to make it through this atlas!"

"I can't wait to see the bright lights of Hoboken," Big Phrank says. "If I can make it there, I can make it anywhere!"

"You know there are lots of other nice places in the United States besides Hoboken and New York City," Tennessee offers. "Miami is a big retirement spot, for instance, and it has a great beach, which you might appreciate, since you're from the desert."

"Where's Miami?" Woodrow asks.

"It's south of New York City, so it's warmer," Tennessee explains.

"I like warmth!" says Woodrow. "I was always very cold when I was alive. I have a glandular problem that keeps me unnaturally thin. And now that I'm a mummy, I get cold even thinking about the cold."

"You and your glands," Phrank spits. "I suppose you want to know where all the best towns in the world are, relative to one another, so you can find the warmest one!"

"That would be nice," says Woodrow. "If it's not too much trouble."

Inter–Activity

Tennessee needs to help Woodrow get a better idea of where the following cities and towns and places are in relation to one another.

1) Using your index, find a map that includes each pair of cities or countries below.

2) Locate each pair of cities or countries on the map (they should be pretty easy to find).

3) Answer the East/West/North/South questions about each pair of cities or countries.

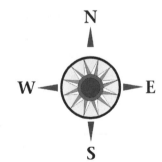

Atlas Map: France
Places: Paris and Lyon

Which is furthest north?
_____

Which is furthest east?
_____

Atlas Map: Russia
Places: Moscow
and St. Petersburg

Which is furthest south?
_____

Which is furthest east?
_____

Atlas Map: South America
Places: Ecuador and Trinidad
and Tobago

Which is furthest east?
_____

Which is furthest south?
_____

Atlas Map: Japan
Places: Yokohama and Osaka

Which is furthest west?
_____

Which is furthest north?
_____

Atlas Map: Europe
Places: Poland and Spain

Which is furthest south?
_____

Which is furthest east?
_____

**Atlas Map: West Indies *or*
Miami, Florida**
Places: Miami, FL and
Havana, Cuba

Which is furthest north?
_____

Which is furthest west?
_____

Atlas Map: South Korea
Places: Seoul and Pusan

Which is furthest north?
_____

Which is furthest west?
_____

HELP GET
TENNESSEE
OUT OF THE
TOMB!

Chamber 1

Chamber 2

Chamber 3
You are
Here

Chamber 4

EXIT!

TOME TEST

Which map in your
atlas gives the
most detail of the
tip of Florida AND Cuba?

1. _____

Which gives the second
most detail?

2. _____

77

RESOURCE
World atlas

SKILL
Reading map coordinates

MAP COORDINATES

I had no idea there were so many great warm places!" Woodrow says delightedly. "Can we change our plans and go to South America, Phrankie?"

"Sure, kid," says Big Phrank. "Have gourd flute, will travel. That's my motto!"

"South America is a big place with lots of different countries in various states of peace and prosperity," Tennessee warns. "You'll want a good map so once you get there, you can decide which place is the best to settle down."

"As long as they love the gourd flute, I couldn't care less!" brags Phrank. "But still, to be on the safe side, why don't you draw us a map with some of the bigger cities on it?"

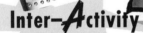 Inter-Activity

For this activity, Tennessee needs you to write the grid coordinates for the following cities in South America.

1) Find the city on the map on the next page.

2) Write the grid coordinate. Remember: Coordinates are written in letter/number order (A3, B2, C6).

Note: Atlases use two ways to pinpoint places on maps for you: (1) grid coordinates and (2) lines of latitude and longitude. ALL atlases use latitude and longitude lines. SOME atlases use grid coordinates. In the atlas's index, they look like this:

Sokoto, Nigeria ... **C6** 13°04'N 5°16'E

Latitude · Grid Coordinate · Longitude

Grid coordinates divide a map into two axes marked by numbers going North/South and letters going East/West. So, in this example, Sokoto, Nigeria, can be found in the box made by the grid coordinate C6.

PLACE	**COORDINATES**	**PLACE**	**COORDINATES**
Asuncion, Paraguay		La Paz, Bolivia	
Buenos Aries, Argentina		Lima, Peru	
Caracas, Venezuela		Paramaribo, Suriname	
Georgetown, Guyana		Santiago, Chile	
Guayaquil, Ecuador		Sao Paulo, Brazil	

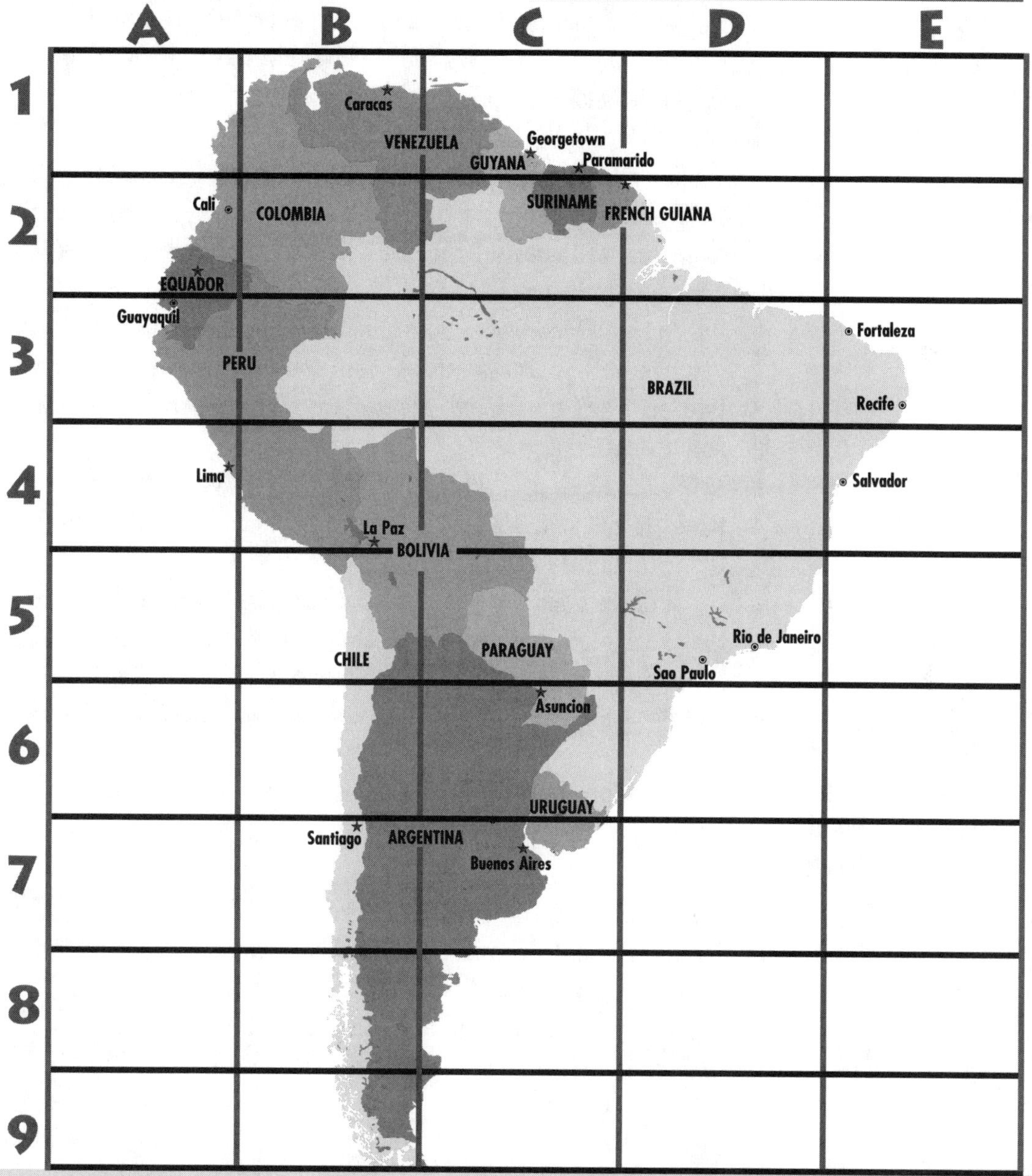

A
B
C
D
E
1
2
3
4
5
6
7
8
9
Caracas
VENEZUELA
Georgetown
GUYANA
Paramarido
SURINAME
FRENCH GUIANA
Cali
COLOMBIA
EQUADOR
Guayaquil
PERU
BRAZIL
Fortaleza
Recife
Lima
Salvador
La Paz
BOLIVIA
CHILE
PARAGUAY
Rio de Janeiro
Sao Paulo
Asuncion
URUGUAY
Santiago
ARGENTINA
Buenos Aires

RESOURCE

World atlas with lines of latitude and longitude

SKILL

Using latitude and longitude lines on a map

LATITUDE AND LONGITUDE 1

Did you all forget something?" says a voice from the corner of the room. Woodrow and Phrank freeze.

"I am right here and I heard everything you said!" Mia Pharaoh laughs. "You are fools! Now that I know you are going to South America, I will track you down and make you pay for your disloyalty!"

"But you're trapped down here forever, right?" Tennessee asks.

"There is one way I can be freed, and that is if my husbands break their Oath of Honesty," the queen explains. "Once they break the oath, I have the power to track them to the ends of the Earth!"

"Uh oh," Woodrow whispers to Phrank. "I didn't know that. We have to change our strategy. She definitely won't be tied up forever. She's a mummy—she can just pull her arm off if she wants and it won't even hurt."

"You're right, pal," Phrank whispers back. "We gotta find more places to hide out. We need a long list of places we *may* go, so Mia can't track us down so easy-like."

"But here's the thing," Woodrow whispers. "We need to know the exact locations so we can meet up in case we get separated."

"Stop whispering!" Mia yells, exasperated. "It's not polite!"

Inter–Activity

Tennessee needs you to give him the latitude and longitude for each of the following places, so Phrank and Woodrow can find each other.

1) Look up the following places in your atlas's index.

2) Copy down the latitude and longitude for each.

Note: Latitude and longitude provide the EXACT location of a spot on ANY map. **Latitude lines** are drawn from east to west around Earth and are numbered by degrees north and south of the equator, which is 0° latitude.

latitude lines

Longitude lines are drawn from north to south around the Earth and numbered by degrees east and west of the prime meridian. The prime meridian passes through the town of Greenwich, England.

Each degree of latitude and longitude is then divided into 60 seconds, so any place on Earth can be labeled and located to within a few hundred yards.

longitude lines

Example:

	LATITUDE	**LONGITUDE**
Memphis, Tenn.	35°07′N	90°03′W
	(degrees) (seconds)	(degrees) (seconds)

<u>Meeting Place</u>	<u>Latitude</u>	<u>Longitude</u>
Amsterdam, Netherlands		
Antananarivo, Madagascar		
Barcelona, Spain		
Casablanca, Morocco		
Greenwich, England		
Kingston, Jamaica		
Melbourne, Australia		
Moscow, Russia		
Rio De Janeiro, Brazil		
South Pole		

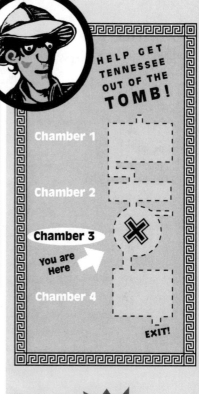

HELP GET TENNESSEE OUT OF THE **TOMB!**

Chamber 1

Chamber 2

Chamber 3
You are Here

Chamber 4

EXIT!

TOME TEST

1) Which two places share the same longitude?

2) Which place is furthest north?

3) Which place is furthest west?

RESOURCE

World atlas with
lines of latitude
and longitude

SKILL

Using latitude and
longitude to locate
places on a map

LATITUDE AND LONGITUDE 2

I've got a good feeling about this," Big Phrank says, holding Tennessee's list of places. "I can see myself reviving interest in the gourd flute in one of these lucky towns."

"Let me see the list," Woodrow says, grabbing for it. "How many of the spots are warm?"

"None of your beeswax, shrimpy," Phrank says, holding the list up high so Woodrow the Small can't reach it. Then, all of a sudden, the list is snatched from his hand by a razor-sharp claw!

"Purrty Kat!" scream the mummy husbands.

The evil feline leads the frantic mummies on a mad chase around the room. "Get that list!" Phrank yells. "Stop that crazy cat!" Woodrow screeches. The exhausted mummies give up and Purrty shows the list to the queen.

"Fumblefingers," Mia laughs and starts reading aloud. "Amsterdam, Netherlands; Antananarivo, Madagascar . . . ."

The husbands take Tennessee aside.

"Give us the latitudes and longitudes of five nice places, but not the names!" Woodrow says. "Mia won't know how to read latitudes and longitudes, since there aren't any marked in her old atlas."

"Good idea, Wood," Phrank agrees. "She'll be looking for us in Antananarivo and we'll be soaking up the sun at 31°19′N, 103°46′W!"

Inter–Activity

Tennessee has provided Woodrow and Phrank with the following five latitudes and longitudes. You need to find out the names of these places.

1) Match the place to the latitude and longitude.

2) Your only hint is the map in your atlas where you can find the place.

Map Hint:
Western Gulf Region U.S.A.
Lat./Long.: 31°19′N, 103°46′W

Place 1: _____

Map Hint:
Indonesia and the Philippines
Lat./Long.: 10°35′S, 105°40′E

Place 2: _____

Map Hint:
West Indies
Lat./Long.: 19°45′N, 73°35′W

Place 3: _____

Map Hint:
Northern Lands and Seas
Lat./Long. 90°00′N, 0°00′?

Place 4: _____

Map Hint:
Australia and New Zealand
Lat./Long. 36°17′S, 148°30′E

Place 5: _____

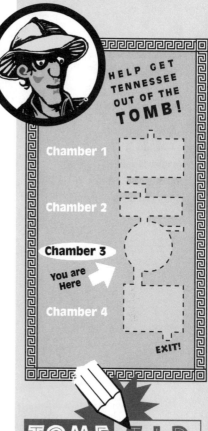

HELP GET TENNESSEE OUT OF THE TOMB!

Chamber 1

Chamber 2

Chamber 3
You are Here

Chamber 4

EXIT!

TOME TIP

Sometimes your atlas will not mark its maps North, South, East and West. If the map isn't marked, you should assume the standard orientation:

North toward the top

South toward the bottom

West to the left

East to the right

RESOURCE

World atlas

A ruler with centimeters

SKILL

Reading a map's legend and converting scale distances

SCALE AND DISTANCE

Phrank drags Mia into a closet.

"Sorry, doll, but I have no choice," he apologizes. "Maybe now you won't eavesdrop!" Phrank rejoins to Woodrow and Tennessee, who are looking over the world atlas.

"The North Pole?" Woodrow says. "That sounds cold!"

"Waddya want?" Phrank retorts. "If you want to be free of this tomb, you're gonna have to make sacrifices! She'll never think to look for us in cold places."

"You're right, Phrankie," Woodrow concedes. "Sometimes I can be so selfish."

"Hey! Tennessee!" Phrank yells. "You don't look so good!"

"So . . . hungry . . ." Tennessee moans.

"Okay, we gotta move fast here. Treasure boy is fading," Phrank says.

"How far away are these places?" Woodrow whines. "I mean, if it's going to be cold, I hope it's a short walk at least."

"Places . . . far . . . away," Tennessee whispers. "Across . . . oceans . . . mountains. You can take airplane . . . ship."

"Are you crazy!" Woodrow screeches. "I'm afraid to float! And you can forget about getting me up in one of those air machines!"

"Aren't there places we can walk to?" Phrank asks. "Like maybe in a neighboring continent or something?"

"Yes," says Tennessee. "Asia."

Inter-Activity

Tennessee has to give the distances between places on the continent of Asia. He needs you to convert the following map measurements to their actual distances.

1) Use your ruler to measure the following distances between the cities.

2) Convert your measurements to the actual distances, using the scales provided.

Map: India
Scale: 1cm = 50 miles
Ratlam to Jamshedpur, India
_____ cm = _____ miles

Jamshedpur

Ratlam

Map: China and Japan
Scale: 1cm = 100 miles
Shanghai, China to Hiroshima, Japan

Hiroshima

Shanghai

_____ cm = _____ miles

Map: Southern Japan
Kurume

Scale: 1 cm = 40 kilometers
Kurume to Yawatahama, Japan

Yawatahama

_____ cm = _____ kilometers

Map: Asia
Scale: 1 cm = 400 kilometers
Moscow, Russia to Hovd, Mongolia

Hovd

Moscow

_____ cm = _____ kilometers

HELP GET TENNESSEE OUT OF THE **TOMB!**

Chamber 1

Chamber 2

Chamber 3

You are Here

Chamber 4

EXIT!

TOME TEST

How far are these U.S. cities from Memphis, Tennessee at the scale 1 cm = 75 miles.

Gadsen, Alabama

3.5 cm = _____

Pontiac, Michigan

9 cm = _____

Boston, Massachusetts

15 cm = _____

RESOURCE
World atlas

SKILL
Recognizing
elevations
and depths

ELEVATION AND DEPTH

That's a lot of walking!" Phrank complains. "I may look like a million cowrie shells, but I'm not in great shape."

"Cowrie shells?" Tennessee asks.

"Ancient Egyptian currency!" Phrank explains.

"Yeah, you couldn't even swim the length of the Nile River," Woodrow agrees. "Maybe I *could* try an airplane or a ship."

"What a pal!" Phrank says, giving Woodrow a big bear hug.

"Good . . . idea," Tennessee stammers. "That would give you . . . more places to choose . . . from."

"Yeah, because I bet there are really tall mountains we would need to climb over and really deep oceans we would have to swim across," Woodrow considers. "And I'm more afraid of heights and depths than I am of sailing and flying."

"Then it's settled," Big Phrank states. "But just to keep Woodrow from changing his mind, maybe you'd better tell us exactly how high the mountains are and how deep the oceans are."

"Okay," Tennessee whispers, as the room starts spinning.

Inter–Activity

Tennessee has to add information about elevations and depths to his maps of regions and places.

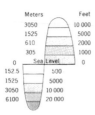

Meters		Feet
3050		10 000
1525		5000
610		2000
305		1000
0	Sea Level	0
152.5		500
1525		5000
3050		10 000
6100		20 000

1) Find the following regional maps and places using the index and table of contents in your atlas.

2) Identify the depth and elevation ranges for the following places on the maps.

Note: Elevation and depth charts accompany each map in your atlas. The chart is also called a *relief*. The relief is usually to the side of the map. It looks like this (left), only in color. It gives elevations and depths in both feet and meters. Each range of elevations (0-200 meters; 4000-6000 meters; etc.) is given a specific color, which corresponds to the elevations on the map that fall into that range.

Map: Southeastern U.S.A. or U.S.A.
Place: Mount Airy, North Carolina in the Blue Ridge Mountains
Lat./Long.: 36°28′N, 80°37′W
Elevation/Depth (in *feet*):
_____

Map: Southeastern U.S.A. or U.S.A.
Place: The Atlantic Ocean, just off the coast of Charleston, South Carolina
Lat./Long.: 32°15′N, 79°00′W
Elevation/Depth (in *feet*):
_____

Map: Atlantic Ocean
Place: The Atlantic Ocean
Lat./Long.: 20°00′N, 35°00′E
Elevation/Depth (in *meters*):
_____

Map: Northern Africa or Africa
Place: Western Sahara
Lat./Long.: 25°05′N, 14°00′W
Elevation/Depth (in *meters*):
_____

Map: Northern Africa or Africa
Place: Algeria: Ahaggar Mountains
Lat./Long.: 23°14′N, 6°00′E
Elevation/Depth (in *feet*):
_____

Map: Northern Africa or Africa
Place: Chad, Tibesti Mountains
Lat./Long.: 20°40′N, 17°48′E
Elevations/Depth (in *meters*):
_____

HELP GET TENNESSEE OUT OF THE TOMB!

Chamber 1

Chamber 2

Chamber 3

You are Here

Chamber 4

EXIT!

TOME TEST

Name the highest peak in the Tibesti Mountains and give its elevation.

_____

_____

Name the highest peak in the Ahaggar Mountains and give its elevation.

_____

_____

RESOURCE

World atlas with a world map showing physical characteristics

SKILL

Reading and interpreting information on a map

WORLD MAPS: PHYSICAL

"Treasure boy!" Phrank yells. "Wake up!"

Tennessee doesn't answer.

"He's dead!" Woodrow screams. "What do we do now!?!"

"I dunno, lemme think," Phrank stalls, pacing the room. "I can't think of anything! Why did they have to take our brains out when they mummified us!"

"Mia will know what to do!" Woodrow panics and races to the closet. He rips open the door, but Mia is gone!

"Uh oh," they say, looking at each other. "Run!"

The mummies escape out a side hallway as Mia strolls into the room, Purrty Kat in her arms.

"You can run, but you cannot hide, boys!" she calls down the hall. "Go get them, Purrty, and bring them back to me."

Mia notices Tennessee passed out on the floor.

"Drat!" she seethes. "I need him to draw me a map of the world so I can find those two dolts should they escape!" She passes a stick of jerky under his nose. Tennessee's eyes flutter open. He gobbles up the jerky and sits up.

"I need a map of the world, and I need it now," the queen says in a threatening manner.

Inter–Activity

Mia Pharaoh demands a physical map of the world so she can find Phrank and Woodrow. Tennessee needs the following information to put the finishing touches on her world map.

1) Find the map of the world's physical characteristics in your atlas. It should be at the front of the atlas, or at the front of the atlas's map section, and it will probably be labeled "World: Physical."

2) Answer the following questions using your physical world map.

Physical World

1) Name the continents intersected by the line of the Tropic of Capricorn. (The Tropic of Capricorn is marked by a dotted line running around Earth below the equator.)

_____

_____

_____

2) Name the continents intersected by the line of the Tropic of Cancer. (The Tropic of Cancer is marked by a dotted line running around Earth above the equator.)

_____

_____

_____

3) Which continents never touch either the Tropic of Cancer or Capricorn?

_____

_____

_____

4) Circle the depth range of the vast majority of the world's oceans:

0-500 feet or **500-10,000 feet** or **10,000-20,000 feet**

5) Name four seas that touch the continent of Europe.

1. _____
2. _____
3. _____
4. _____

6) Which ocean separates Africa from Australia?

_____

7) Which ocean separates Australia and South America?

_____

8) Which continent is found completely above 30°00'N latitude?

_____

9) Which continent reaches furthest north, South America or Africa?

_____

10) Which continents are intersected by 70°00'W longitude?

_____

_____

_____

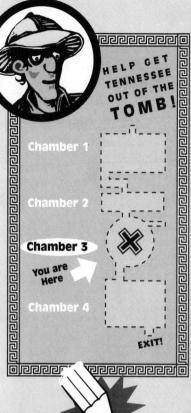

HELP GET TENNESSEE OUT OF THE **TOMB!**

Chamber 1

Chamber 2

Chamber 3

You are Here

Chamber 4

EXIT!

TOME TIP

There are all kinds of ways to project the globe on a flat surface. Here are two:

Sinusoidal

Homosline

RESOURCE

World atlas with a political world map

SKILL

Reading and interpreting information on a map

WORLD MAPS: POLITICAL

How did you escape?" Tennessee asks the queen.

"Purrty Kat scratched through my bonds," Mia Pharaoh explains. "She hates my husbands and would never let them outsmart me."

"Oh. Well, thanks for the food," says Tennessee.

"I only fed you so you could finish up my maps, and I am glad I did," Mia replies. "I am very impressed with what the modern world looks like. So diverse! It has given me a new goal."

"What's that?" Tennessee asks innocently.

"Total world domination!" Mia cackles. "If ruling Egypt with an iron fist was fun, I can only imagine what ruling the entire planet will be like!"

"You want to rule the world?" Tennessee asks.

"Exactly," she says. "And after you provide me with a political map of all of the countries on the planet, I will."

Tennessee has had just about enough of crazy mummies. He needs to get out of this tomb!

"Okay okay, no problem," he relents. "But where did you get that jerky? I thought Purrty Kat ate it all."

She shows him her left hand—there are only four fingers left.

Tennessee passes out and Mia Pharaoh howls with evil laughter.

Inter–Activity

When Tennessee wakes up, he needs to draw Mia Pharaoh a good political world map to accompany her physical world map.

1) Find the map of the world's nations in your atlas. It should be near the physical world map at the front of the atlas, or at the front of the atlas's map section, and it will probably be labeled "World: Political."

2) Answer the following questions, using your atlas's political world map.

Political World

1) What is the southernmost country on the continent of Africa?

_____

2) What is the westernmost country on the continent of South America?

_____

3) What country shares the United States's southern border?

_____

4) What is the northernmost country on the continent of Asia?

_____

5) Which sea separates Egypt and Turkey?

_____

6) Which country separates India from Afghanistan?

_____

7) Do China and India share a border?

_____

8) Do Angola and Tanzania share a border?

_____

9) Which country is furthest east, China or Japan?

_____

10) Which country is furthest west, Nigeria or Sudan?

_____

11) Which countries in South America are intersected by the equator?

_____

_____

_____

12) Which sea separates North and South Korea from Japan?

_____

13) Which country is off the southeast coast of Greenland?

_____

HELP GET TENNESSEE OUT OF THE TOMB!

Chamber 1

Chamber 2

Chamber 3

You are Here

Chamber 4

EXIT!

TOME TEST

Which continent has the most countries touching the equator?

_____

Which countries lie on the equator?

_____

_____

_____

RESOURCE

World atlas
with geographical
information

SKILL

Using thematic maps

BEYOND THE MAPS 1

hat use do I have for the ring finger on my left hand?" Mia asks the revived explorer. "I will never marry again."

"I just wish you would have told me before I ate it," says Tennessee, sticking out his tongue.

"There was no time. You were at death's door," the queen explains. "Plus Purrty Kat thought it would be funny. And she was right!"

"Real funny," Tennessee mutters.

"Anyway, the new maps in my atlas are fantastic," the queen continues. "I commend you for your excellent work, even if much of it was done at the request of my traitor husbands."

"So can I do your Dangerous Puzzle of Pain now?" Tennessee begs.

"No," Mia answers. "I need to know more about the world. I know where everything is, thanks to your maps, but now I need to know how Earth works. Tides, rainfall, ice caps—the ruler of the planet needs to know about these things if she is to rule effectively."

"What do you mean?" asks Tennessee, reeling.

"For instance, if I want to banish my enemies to a humid, hilly region, I need to know if such a region exists," she explains.

"If you say so," says the weary explorer.

"Oh I know so, intruder!" Mia Pharaoh barks. "Knowledge is power! Do not ever forget that!"

Inter–Activity

Tennessee needs to create a section in Mia Pharaoh's atlas that covers Earth's geographical and geological make-up in detail.

1) Turn to your atlas's section on world geography. Sometimes the section is called "World Thematic Maps" because the maps convey information on all sorts of different themes, like agriculture and languages.

2) Find the following categories/maps.

3) Answer the true/false questions for each section.

World Geography Thematic Maps

1) Currents in the Atlantic Ocean between North America and Europe move in a circular motion.

true or false

2) Ice drifts in the Antarctic stop right around longitude 60°00's.

true or false

3) The Pacific Plate is drifting away from North America.

true or false

4) The Eurasian and African Plates share both *convergent* and *transformative* boundaries.

true or false

5) The western edge of North America has an alpine system with mountains and plains.

true or false

6) There are currently ice caps on Greenland and Antarctica.

true or false

7) A large, northern portion of South America gets over 40 inches of rain from November 1–April 30 each year.

true or false

8) The winds in the Indian Ocean off Africa and Asia reverse direction between January and July.

true or false

9) A hilly, humid region stretches across the Indian peninsula on the Asian continent.

true or false

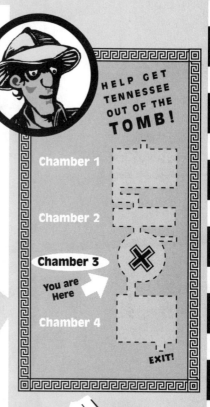

HELP GET TENNESSEE OUT OF THE TOMB!

Chamber 1

Chamber 2

Chamber 3

You are Here

Chamber 4

EXIT!

TOME TIP

Your atlas's thematic maps provide all kinds of statistics on things like population, agriculture, health, and natural resources. The thematic maps are great places to look for information for all different kinds of research papers, even if the paper has nothing to do with geography.

RESOURCE
World atlas with
thematic maps

SKILL
Interpreting data on
thematic maps

BEYOND THE MAPS 2

"Excellent," says the queen. "A hilly, humid region stretches across a southern portion of the Asian continent. The perfect place to banish my enemies!"

"And who might those enemies be?" Tennessee asks.

"Oh, anyone who gets in my way," Mia considers. "Anyone who hates cats. Anyone who has invaded a mummy's tomb. Anyone who likes a cold climate. Anyone whose name starts with the letter *c*."

"The letter *c*?" Tennessee asks.

"Yes, *c* for *chihuahua*, the dog that bit me when I was a child," Mia explains. "All of these people will learn to fear humid hills."

"How are you going to find these people?" Tennessee asks.

"I will start by making sure my atlas has lots of information about the world's human population!" Mia orders. "So get to it!"

"I refuse!" Tennessee barks. "I will not help you take over the planet!"

"Fine, I do not need you," Mia says. "I can figure it out myself once I get out there. Prepare to die, intruder!"

"Wait wait!" Tennessee counters. "I changed my mind. Let me get to work."

Tennessee realizes that he is the only thing standing between Mia Pharaoh and world domination. He has to play along until he can figure out a way to foil her plans.

Inter—Activity

Tennessee needs to create a section in Mia Pharaoh's atlas that covers in detail what humans are doing on—and to—the planet.

1) Turn to your atlas's section on world populations. (Sometimes the section is called "World Thematic Maps" because the maps convey information on all sorts of different themes, like agriculture and languages.)

2) Find the following categories/maps.

3) Answer the true/false questions for each section.

World Population Thematic Maps

Population

1) Population density in Europe is generally less than population density in Australia.

    true or false

2) Greenland is mostly uninhabited.

    true or false

Languages

3) South Americans speak mostly Uralian and Paleosiberian languages.

    true or false

4) Asia's languages include Turkic, Tungus-Manchu, Mongolic, Chinese, and Slavic.

    true or false

Health and Life Expectancy

5) India has fewer physicians per person than China.

    true or false

6) Life expectancy in both China and India is 60-70 years.

    true or false

Agriculture

7) There is a lot of livestock ranching in the western half of North America.

    true or false

8) All of Australia is a fertile, agricultural area.

    true or false

Energy Production and Consumption

9) The United States produces more energy than it consumes.

    true or false

10) Russia produces more energy than it consumes.

    true or false

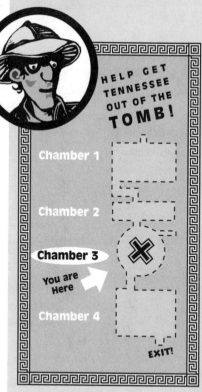

HELP GET TENNESSEE OUT OF THE TOMB!

Chamber 1

Chamber 2

Chamber 3

You are Here

Chamber 4

EXIT!

TOME TEST

Which country is host to the greatest percentage of the world's refugees?

WORLD ATLAS

RESOURCE
World atlas

SKILL
Using the whole
world atlas

MIA PHARAOH'S DANGEROUS PUZZLE OF PAIN

3

"Meow!" Purrty Kat announces, nudging Phrank and Woodrow from the side hall toward the queen.

"You have betrayed me!" the queen yells at her shivering husbands. "But I will let you out of the tomb anyway. Why? I need you both if I am to rule the world!"

Phrank the Large, and Woodrow the Small smile at each other while Tennessee works on this treacherous puzzle, fearful for the fate of the human race.

Inter-Activity

1) Complete Mia Pharaoh's Dangerous Puzzle of Pain, using your atlas to fill in the word puzzle.

2) When you have completed the word puzzle, fill in the Extra Dangerous Password.

ACROSS

1- the European language likely spoken by someone living at 50°00'N, 10°00'E
4 - world's largest ocean
5 - major Russian city at 55°45'N 37°37'E
6 - according to the map legend, which Latvian town is smaller, Liepaja or Aizpute?
7 - river flowing into the Gulf of Owan near Gwadar, Pakistan
9 - the only continent that doesn't end in an "a"
12 - country with 2nd highest percentage refugee population
14 - country that borders both Bolivia and Ecuador
15 - Australian archipelago at 20°15'S 116°25'E
16 - _____ River; one of two rivers flowing into James Bay near Moosonee, Canada (begins with "A")
17 - town just north of Punxsutawney, PA
20 - U.S. state at 34°00'N 93°00'W
21 - Erg _____, a desert area stretching through northern Mauritania and Western Algeria
22 - town in Norway at 64°28'N 11°14'E
23 - _____ Republic, shares a border with Haiti

DOWN

2 - sound made by the animals ranched across the United States' Midwest and on South America's eastern border
3 - country sharing Spain's western border
4 - _____ tectonics
5 - sea separating Europe and Africa
8 - in the U.S.A., is a person over age 85 less likely to be a <u>he</u> or a <u>she</u>?
10 - island nation between Tanzania and Madagascar
11 - mountain range crossing Slovakia, Ukraine, and Romania
13 - state with the town Loogootee at 38°40'N 86°55'W
14 - largest city in Arizona
18 - country in Southeast Asia with the highest population density
19 - U.S. protectorate island about 1,000 miles due east of the Philippines

EXTRA DANGEROUS
PASSWORD QUESTION 3

What do the letters in the linked blocks spell?

Password 3

_____

Tennessee listens to Mia Pharaoh tell her husbands about her evil plan.

The first part is particularly cunning: she has no army, so instead of invading countries, she wants to make a big splash by publishing her autobiography, *Me: A Pharaoh*. In it she will reveal a happy, cat-filled childhood, her battles with weight (solved by mummification), and her Seven Golden Rules to Ruling Success.

She'll go on all the talk shows, become a household name, sell the statues of her husbands to raise campaign funds, then run for president of the United States with talk show host Oprah Winfrey as her vice president. She'll make Tennessee her spokesperson, install Phrank and Woodrow as the leaders of the U.S. Army and Navy, and then grab control of the world!

Tennessee needs to get out alive now so he can warn everyone. He has no food and is floating in and out of consciousness. He reads through Mia's autobiography quickly. It's very repetitive, plus it needs its final chapter where she explains why a mummy should be president.

Tennessee grabs Mia's thesaurus so he can get started on Mia's autobiography. It's in even worse shape than her book! He'll need a lot of help.

Me: A Pharaoh

AUTOBIOGRAPHY

THESAURUS

Prepare for the fourth chamber of Mia Pharaoh's Gauntlet of Giant Tomes!

Chamber 1

Chamber 2

Chamber 3

Chamber 4

You are Here

EXIT!

FOR STARTERS

Spend some quality time with your thesaurus, especially its Synopsis of Categories. Did you know there were this many categories of words in the English language?

THESAURUS

RESOURCE

Thesaurus with a
synopsis of categories

SKILL

Using the synopsis
of categories

WORD CATEGORIES

So what do you think of *Me: A Pharaoh?*" Mia Pharaoh asks nervously. "Is it any good?"

"Well, it's very *interesting*," says Tennessee diplomatically. "For example, I had no idea you were raised by cats until the age of three."

"Yes, my country was being attacked by foreign invaders, so my parents thought sneaking me out of the palace along with their cat's new litter of kittens was a good idea."

"How did they do that?" Tennessee asks.

"They pasted a pair of cloth ears on my head, drew whiskers on my face, and stuck a feather duster that looked like a tail out of the back of my diaper. It is all in the book!"

"Oh, I'm sorry," Tennessee apologizes. "The writing was so repetitive that, after a while, I got so bored I couldn't read anymore."

"Then you missed the part about Purrty Kat being my sister!" screams the outraged queen. "That is the most important part of Chapter 1!"

"Your sister!" Tennessee exclaims. "That explains a lot!"

"I need this to be a bestseller!" Mia yells. "Make my book less boring!"

Inter-Activity

Luckily, Mia Pharaoh's book has chapter titles that match the word classes in the synopsis of categories in your thesaurus. Tennessee needs you to get information from your thesaurus's synopsis of categories.

1) Turn to your thesaurus's synopsis of categories. (It will be listed in the table of contents.)

2) For each chapter title (word class), write down three word categories that you think would be most helpful in making Mia's autobiography less boring.

Chapter 1:
The Body and the Senses

_____

_____

Chapter 2: Feelings

_____

_____

Chapter 3:
Place and Change of Place

_____

_____

Chapter 4:
Measure and Shape

_____

_____

Chapter 5:
Living Things

_____

_____

Chapter 6:
Natural Phenomena

_____

_____

Chapter 7:
Behavior and Will

_____

_____

Chapter 8: Language

_____

_____

Chapter 9:
Human Society and
Institutions

_____

_____

Chapter 10:
Values and Ideals

_____

_____

Chapter 11: Arts

_____

_____

Chapter 12:
Occupations and Crafts

_____

_____

Chapter 13:
Sports and Amusements

_____

_____

Chapter 14: The Mind and Ideas

_____

_____

_____

Chapter 15:
Science and Technology

_____

_____

_____

HELP GET
TENNESSEE
OUT OF THE
TOMB!

Chamber 1

Chamber 2

Chamber 3

Chamber 4

You are
Here

EXIT!

TOME TEST

How many different
kinds of words
(categories) does
your thesaurus divide the
English language into?

_____

What are the first
and last categories
in your thesaurus?

First Category:

_____

Last Category:

_____

THESAURUS

RESOURCE
Thesaurus

SKILL
Finding synonyms by
using the index

USING THE INDEX

"I think I have some good stuff to work with now," Tennessee says. "Now I just need to find some synonyms for them so I don't just repeat the same words over and over."

"What are synonyms?" Mia asks.

"A synonym is a word that means the same thing or close to the same thing as another word," Tennessee explains. "A thesaurus is full of them. Unfortunately, Woodrow made up all of the synonyms in *your* thesaurus."

"So sue me!" Woodrow defends.

"You obviously have a very high opinion of yourself, queen," Tennessee continues.

"I am the cat's meow," Mia agrees.

"So I need to find synonyms for all of your complimentary comments about yourself."

"I have some ideas!" Phrank the Large butts in. "How about *aces*, and *hubba hubba*, and *you take the cake*."

"Those are all . . . *interesting*," Tennessee says. "But I'll also need some synonyms that are more commonly used, so people who read her book know what she's talking about."

"Good thinking!" Phrank bellows. "You are *aces*, Tennessee Toledo, *aces!*"

Inter–Activity

Tennessee needs some synonyms for Mia Pharaoh's most overused words.

1) Turn to your thesaurus's index. (It will be listed in the table of contents.)

2) Find each of the overused words from Mia Pharaoh's memoir provided on the next page.

3) Copy down the first two synonym types listed in the index.

4) Copy down the word category.paragraph number for each synonym type.

Note: Words are listed alphabetically in your thesaurus's index. Once you find the word in the index, you will notice that your thesaurus does NOT give a page number to find it on. Instead, it gives category.paragraph numbers for the word or its synonyms, like this:

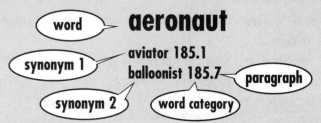

word → **aeronaut**

synonym 1 → aviator 185.1
synonym 2 → balloonist 185.7 ← paragraph
word category

This entry listing tells you that you can find synonyms for **aeronaut** in the sense meaning "aviator" in category 185, paragraph 1. It also tells you that synonyms for **aeronaut** in the sense meaning "balloonist" are in category 185, paragraph 7.

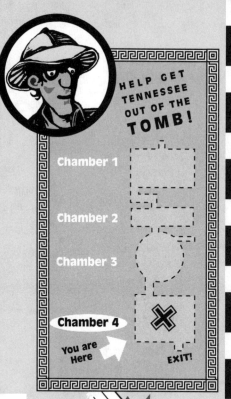

HELP GET TENNESSEE OUT OF THE **TOMB!**

Chamber 1

Chamber 2

Chamber 3

Chamber 4

You are Here

EXIT!

	Two Synonyms	Category.Paragraph
beautiful	1. _____	_____
	2. _____	_____
intelligent	1. _____	_____
	2. _____	_____
strong	1. _____	_____
	2. _____	_____
faithful	1. _____	_____
	2. _____	_____
independent	1. _____	_____
	2. _____	_____
money	1. _____	_____
	2. _____	_____
power	1. _____	_____
	2. _____	_____

TOME TIP

The terminology in a thesaurus can get a little confusing. To review:

WORD CLASS
Words are grouped into 15 large classes.

WORD CATEGORY
The 15 word classes are divided into 1075 categories.

CATEGORY PARAGRAPH
The 1075 word categories are each divided into paragraphs of similar synonyms.

THESAURUS

RESOURCE
Thesaurus

SKILL
Finding
"everyday"
synonyms

FINDING SYNONYMS 1

All done," says Tennessee. "I think your best shot at getting on the talk shows is to highlight your Seven Golden Rules for Ruling Success."

"Great idea, intruder," says Mia. "It will give people a taste of what is to come."

"The problem is, your seven steps aren't very catchy," Tennessee explains. "We need to use simple words that people use every day, so they can better remember what you wrote."

"Are you sure?" Mia asks.

"It works for Oprah Winfrey," Tennessee says.

Inter–Activity

Tennessee needs you to find everyday synonyms for some of the words in *Me: A Pharaoh's Seven Golden Rules for Ruling Success.*

1) Look up the **bold-faced** words.

2) Replace the **bold-faced** words with everyday synonyms.

3) Rewrite the rule with your synonyms. Does it sound better now? Does it sound familiar?

Note: Here are a few rules for picking a good synonym:

1) Pick a word you have heard of before. Words that aren't commonly used are usually NOT the best synonym.

2) Read the sentence aloud with the synonym you picked. If it sounds right, stick with it. If it sounds weird, try a new synonym.

3) Trust your instincts. If you think the word is a good synonym, it *probably* is.

4) If you have no clue, pick the shorter word. It is *probably* used more often in conversation and writing than a longer synonym.

Mia Pharaoh's Seven Golden Rules for Ruling Success

These are the seven rules I followed when ruling Egypt.

1. Never **permit** _____ them to see you **perspire** _____ .
New Rule: _____

2. The **crayon** _____ is mightier than the **saber** _____ .
New Rule: _____

3. Don't put the **conveyance** _____ before the **equine** _____ .
New Rule: _____

4. If it's not **busted** _____ , don't **repair** _____ it.
New Rule: _____

5. **Intimates** _____ may come and go, but **kin-folk** _____ is forever.
New Rule: _____

6. He who **chortles** _____ last **guffaws** _____ longest.
New Rule: _____

7. **Separate** _____ and **vanquish** _____ !
New Rule: _____

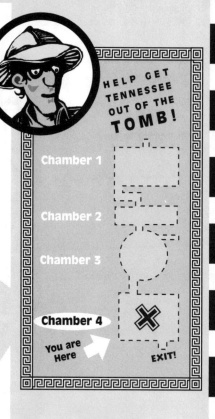

HELP GET TENNESSEE OUT OF THE **TOMB!**

Chamber 1

Chamber 2

Chamber 3

Chamber 4

You are Here

EXIT!

TOME TEST

Find a nonformal synonym for the following words. Nonformal synonyms are marked either <nf> or <nonformal> in your thesaurus.

Word	Nonformal synonym
false alarm	_____
consent	_____

THESAURUS

FINDING SYNONYMS 2

"I'm done editing your autobiography!" Tennessee exclaims with pure joy. "Let me at that Dangerous Puzzle of Pain!"

"Not so fast, treasure boy," Phrank says. "Woodrow and I have a bone to pick with you. And with you, queenie!"

"Whatever could be the problem?" Mia asks.

"We found an old copy of your autobiography," Woodrow explains. "And we happened to read a certain chapter where you describe your dearly departed husbands! How dare you paint us in such a bad light! Unless you change this chapter, the deal is off! We will not help you rule the world! We'll stay right here in this tomb and you'll be one lonely mummy."

"Plus, I'm gonna smash our statues into itty bitty bits !" Phrank adds. "How do you like them apples?"

"Just relax, you two!" Mia says. "I am sure Tennessee has already made changes in that chapter so that you do not come off as a couple of bumbling idiots, right Tennessee?"

"Um yeah, just a minute," Tennessee says, wondering if he will ever see the light of day again.

Inter–Activity

To make Phrank and Woodrow happy, Tennessee needs you to find the opposite of the bold-faced words in the following paragraphs about Little Woodrow and Big Phrank.

1) Write down the exact opposite of the highlighted words.

2) Find a good synonym for each of your new words.

3) Put the synonym in the blank for Tennessee, so he can "revise" the Phrank and Woodrow chapter.

Excerpt from
Me: A Pharaoh

Little Woodrow

My first husband was Little Woodrow. At first, his jokes made me laugh. After a while, they made me **tired**. He talked with a **weird** accent, he was **always** worrying, he was always **sick**, and he couldn't keep his eyes off other women. Once, I found him kissing my best friend Cleopatra! That's when I knew I had to **divorce** him. Lucky for him, he died first.

Word	Opposite	Synonym
tired		
weird		
always		
sick		
divorce		

Big Phrank

My second husband was Big Phrank. He was much older than I was, and very **ugly**. His hair was **thin**, his belly was **huge**, and his taste in clothes was **terrible**. So why did I marry him? He was rich and famous. He had been a great entertainer in his youth. His nickname was Chairman of the Gourd, because he played the gourd flute like a dream. When I married him, his career was really **over**.

Word	Opposite	Synonym
ugly		
thin		
huge		
terrible		
over		

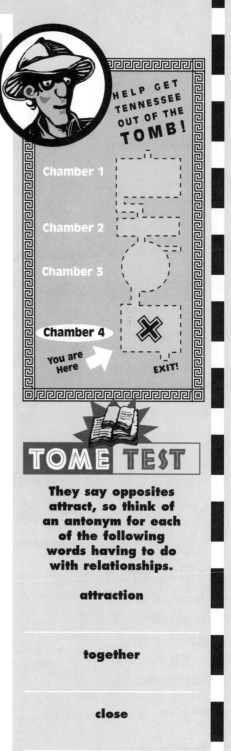

HELP GET TENNESSEE OUT OF THE **TOMB!**

Chamber 1

Chamber 2

Chamber 3

Chamber 4

You are Here

EXIT!

TOME TEST

They say opposites attract, so think of an antonym for each of the following words having to do with relationships.

attraction

together

close

THESAURUS

MIA PHARAOH'S DANGEROUS PUZZLE OF PAIN 4

"That's better," says Phrank the Large. "Now we are being treated with the respect we deserve. Right, Wood?"

"Right, Phrankie," Woodrow agrees. "Respect!"

"Then our work here is done, my husbands," Mia says wistfully, picking up Purrty Kat. "Say good-bye to the ancient tomb. The modern world awaits!"

"Aces!" Phrank exclaims. "Gimme that army!"

"Yeah, good!" Woodrow screeches. "Anchors away!"

"The intruder just has to use my thesaurus to put the finishing touches on my final chapter," Mia explains. "Then we will rule the world with talk show host Oprah Winfrey!"

"Okay," Tennessee exhales. "I think I have just enough strength left."

Mia Pharaoh, Phrank the Large, Woodrow the Small, and Purrty Kat give each other high fives and pats on the back as Tennessee slogs through the queen's final chapter.

"Ouch! Purrty!" whines Woodrow. "You scratched me!"

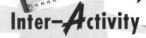

Inter-Activity

Tennessee needs to add the exact right synonyms to Mia Pharaoh's last chapter.

1) Fill in the blanks in Mia Pharaoh's chapter, using your thesaurus and the hints provided below.

2) When you are done, answer Mia Pharaoh's Extra Dangerous Password Question.

Chapter 16: Why I Should Rule the World

So, people of the **modern** world, as you can see, my Seven Golden Rules for Ruling Success are **applicable** to contemporary society. I do not think it would be inaccurate to state that the world would be a better place if I was given the **opportunity** to **rule**, as I was given in Egypt 5,000 years ago.

Some may argue that I was too **imperious** as a pharaoh. I would have to disagree. By eliminating my **enemies**, I was doing the world a favor. No one gains from those who would harm the pharaoh, so it is best those people are eliminated. By invading foreign lands and **subjugating** their peoples, I was merely serving the greater good: ever-increasing riches for myself. And by elevating **cats** to positions of power, I assured that other species were represented in my government. The cat is a friend to all animals!

Except dogs. Maybe you are afraid for dear old Rover and cute little Toto? If so, on this single point, I am willing to **compromise**. I hereby promise that, if you elect me your ruler, I will not turn any dogs into goldfish. Read my lips: no new goldfish.

Thank you for reading my **book**. On behalf of my dead husbands Woodrow the Small and Phrank the Large, and my sister Purrty Kat, I look forward to ruling over you with an iron fist.

Clues

1. modern, *synonym*, c _ _ _ _ _ _ _ _ _ _ _; the noun form of this word is also a main synonym for *coeval*.

2. applicable, *synonym*, r _ _ _ _ _ _ _; kind of rhymes with *elephant*.

3. opportunity, *synonym*, c _ _ _ _ _; also a synonym for *gamble*.

4. rule, *nonformal synonym*, c _ _ _ t _ _ s _ _ _ _ ; something a basketball play-by-play man also does.

5. imperious, *nonformal synonym*, b _ _ _ _ ; rhymes with *mossy*.

6. enemies, *synonym, plural form*, f _ _ _;

as in "Fee Fi _ _; Fum, I smell the blood of an Englishman!"

7. subjugating, *synonym*, c _ _ _ _ _ _ _ _ _; think of the phrase "Divide and _ _ _ _ _ _ _ _."
(See Mia Pharaoh's Seventh Golden Rule.)

8. cats, *nonformal synonym, plural form*, k _ _ _ _ - c _ _; the cute way of saying *cats*.

9. compromise, *nonformal synonym*, m _ _ _ a d _ _ _; something game show host Monty Hall did for 20-odd years.

10. book, *synonym*, t _ _ _; Gauntlet of Giant _ _ _ _ _ _ (singular form).

EXTRA DANGEROUS PASSWORD QUESTION 4

What is a four-letter synonym for *final* that rhymes with *past*?

Password 4

_____

TENNESSEE

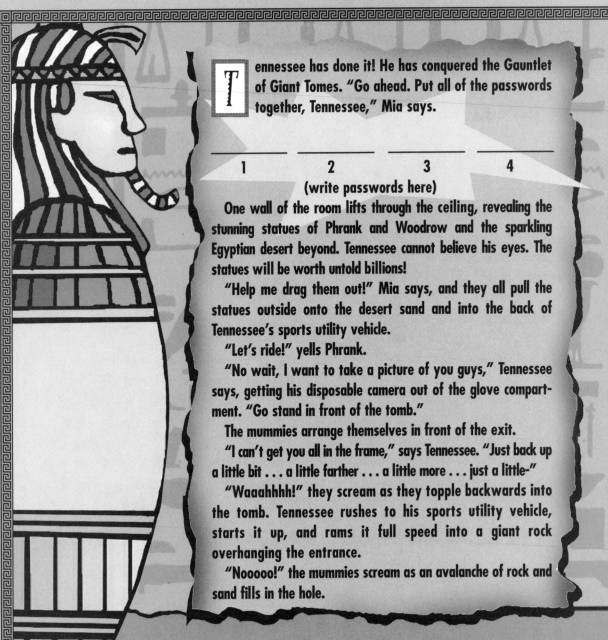

ennessee has done it! He has conquered the Gauntlet of Giant Tomes. "Go ahead. Put all of the passwords together, Tennessee," Mia says.

_____ _____ _____ _____
1   2   3   4

(write passwords here)

One wall of the room lifts through the ceiling, revealing the stunning statues of Phrank and Woodrow and the sparkling Egyptian desert beyond. Tennessee cannot believe his eyes. The statues will be worth untold billions!

"Help me drag them out!" Mia says, and they all pull the statues outside onto the desert sand and into the back of Tennessee's sports utility vehicle.

"Let's ride!" yells Phrank.

"No wait, I want to take a picture of you guys," Tennessee says, getting his disposable camera out of the glove compartment. "Go stand in front of the tomb."

The mummies arrange themselves in front of the exit.

"I can't get you all in the frame," says Tennessee. "Just back up a little bit . . . a little farther . . . a little more . . . just a little-"

"Waaahhhh!" they scream as they topple backwards into the tomb. Tennessee rushes to his sports utility vehicle, starts it up, and rams it full speed into a giant rock overhanging the entrance.

"Nooooo!" the mummies scream as an avalanche of rock and sand fills in the hole.

ESCAPES

"Woo hoo!" Tennessee yells. "I did it! I foiled Mia Pharaoh's evil plan!"

He reaches deep into the glove compartment for his extra store of turkey jerky and drives into the sunset with his priceless statues, already thinking about his next adventure . . . .

THE END

Read This First

You can do the Inter-Activities in this book with ANY reference book. BUT—and this is a very big BUT—if you use reference books that are different from the ones we recommend, your answers will often not match up exactly with the answers in the back of this book. THIS IS NOT THAT BIG A DEAL. The important thing is you get to know your reference books, no matter what brand they are. But if you want to be able to check your answers, by all means, use a recent copy of the WORLD ALMANAC AND BOOK OF FACTS, GOODE'S WORLD ATLAS: 20TH EDITION, MERRIAM WEBSTER'S COLLEGIATE DICTIONARY: 10TH EDITION, and ROGET'S INTERNATIONAL THESAURUS: 6TH EDITION.

Read This Second

Some of the Tome Tests ask you for personal information, like your favorite foods, or who YOU would vote the next Miss America. For those questions, Tennessee has given his answers, but yours will probably be different (unless you also think Tennessee's girlfriend should be Miss America!)

Chamber 1
World Almanac

(Using *The World Almanac and Book of Facts 2002*)

Almanac Subjects
p.18

Aerospace
Agriculture
Arts and Media
Associations and
  Societies
Astronomy
Awards—Medals—
  Prizes
Buildings, Bridges, and
  Tunnels
Cities of the U.S.
Computers and the
  Internet
Consumer Information
Crime
Disasters
Economics
Education
Employment
Energy
Environment
Flags and Maps
General Index
Health
Historical Figures
Language
Meteorology
National Defense
Nations of the World
Noted Personalities
Postal Information
Presidents of the United
  States
Presidential Elections
Quick Reference Index
Religion
Science and Technology
Social Security
Special Feature: Focus
  on Children
Sports
State and Local
  Government
States and other Areas
  of the U.S.
Taxes
Telecommunications
Trade and
  Transportation
Travel and Tourism
United States Facts
United States
  Government
United States History
United States
  Population
Vital Statistics
Weights and Measures
World Exploration and
  Geography
World History
Year in Pictures
Year In Review

Tome Test

Health: There are 5,800 licensed acupuncturists in the U.S.

Using the Index
p.20

TEN SUBJECTS COVERED IN DETAIL
(Your list may be different)

1. Art
2. Children
3. Elections, U.S.
4. Health and medicine
5. Men
6. Religion
7. Spain
8. States, U.S.
9. Washington, D.C.
10. Women

FIVE FACTS ABOUT U.S. ELECTIONS

1. The Speaker of the House makes $186,300 annually.

2. Bob Dole was the Senate majority leader from 1995-6.

3. James K. Polk was Speaker of the House from 1835-9.

4. New York elects 31 representatives to the House of Representatives.

5. Strom Thurmond (R-SC) was first elected to the senate in 1956.

Tome Test
Treasure Hunters. Because I, Tennessee Toledo, want to become a famous treasure hunter.

Reading Tables
p.22
(Your state and statistics may be different)

State: Tennessee

1.
Table Title
U.S. Public High School Graduation Rates 1998-99
State Statistic
59.9% graduate

2.
Table Title
Persons in Poverty, by State, 1989, 1999
State Statistic
12.7% in poverty in 1999

3.
Table Title
Presidential Election Returns 2000
State Statistic
Bush beat Gore by almost 100,000 votes

4.
Table Title
Key Data for the 50 States
State Statistic
Entered the Union June 1, 1796

Year in Review
p.24
(Your year and events may be different)

Year: 2001

Date: February 9, 2001
Event: Nine people die when a surfacing U.S. submarine hits a Japanese fishing boat.

Date: April 1, 2001
Event: China holds the crew of a U.S. spy plane eleven days after it crashes in China.

Date: June 11, 2001
Event: Timothy McVeigh is executed for killing 168 people when he bombed a federal office building in Oklahoma City, OK in 1995.

Date: June 15, 2001
Event: L.A. Lakers win their second NBA title in a row.

Date: July 8, 2001
Event: Venus Williams wins her second consecutive Wimbledon single's title.

Date: August 22, 2001
Event: Senator Jesse Helms announces he is retiring.

Date: March 25, 2001
Event: *Gladiator* wins the Oscar for best picture.

Date: September 11, 2001
Event: Terrorists hijack and crash four U.S. planes into U.S. landmarks, killing thousands of people.

Tome Test
Tennessee's Birthday: 9/29
Event Date: 9/29/2001

Event: Taliban leader Mullah Omar refuses to hand over Osama Bin Laden.

Presidential Elections
p.26

PRESIDENTIAL ELECTIONS

1936
Candidate 1
Franklin Roosevelt
Party
Democratic
Popular Vote Total
27,751,597
Candidate 2
Alfred Landon
Party
Republican
Popular Vote Total
16,679,583

1996
Candidate 1
Bill Clinton
Party
Democratic
Popular Vote Total
47,401,185
Candidate 2
Bob Dole
Party
Republican
Popular Vote Total
39,197,469

1984
Candidate 1
Walter Mondale
Party
Democratic
Popular Vote Total
37,457,215
Candidate 2
Ronald Reagan
Party
Republican
Popular Vote Total
54,281,858

1956
Candidate 1
Dwight Eisenhower
Party
Republican
Popular Vote Total
35,585,316
Candidate 2

(Adlai Stevenson)
Party
Democratic
Popular Vote Total
26,031,322

1928
Candidate 1
(Alfred Smith)
Party
Democratic
Popular Vote Total
15,016,443
Candidate 2
Herbert Hoover
Party
Republican
Popular Vote Total
21,392,190

How many of these LOSERS were Democrats? 3

Which LOSER lost by the most votes? Walter Mondale

Which WINNER received the FEWEST votes? Herbert Hoover

Tome Test
1964 winner: Lyndon Johnson
1864 winner: Abraham Lincoln
1972 loser: George McGovern
1872 loser: Horace Greeley

Economic Statistics
p.28

1. Services
2. Finance, insurance, real estate
3. $10 bill: Hamilton
   $100 bill: Franklin
   $1,000 bill: Cleveland
4. 2002
5. Oklahoma, New Mexico, Arizona, Alaska, Hawaii

6. United Kingdom
7. Luxembourg

Tome Test
2000 Total:
81,900,000 troy ounces
Biggest producer: South Africa

Annual Stats and Facts
p.30

Dog Show
1. Breed: English Springer Spaniel
2. Rank: 26
3. No. Champion Wendessa Crown Prince is a Pekingese. That breed was ranked 29 in 2000.
4. No
5. Yes, a Bichon Frises won in 2001.
6. One
7. Three types of terriers
8. Norwich, Scottish, and Fox Terriers

Tome Test
Tennessee's choice:
Loteki Supernatural Being
(1999 Best-in-show)

Statistical Overviews
p.32
(Your states and statistics may be different.)

	TENNESSEE	GEORGIA
High school graduation rates (1998-99)	59.9%	55.8%
Number of public libraries (1998)	288	367
SAT mean verbal scores (2001)	562	491
Average ACT score (2000-01)	20.0	19.9
Math Achievement Grade 8 (% of students scoring at or above basic level in 2000)	53%	56%
Reading Achievement Grade 8 (% of students scoring at or above basic level in 1998)	26%	25%
Science Achievement Grade 8 (% of students scoring at or above basic level in 1996)	22%	21%
Expenditure per Pupil (fall 1998)	$5,521	$6,534

Education Overview
More of Tennessee's students graduate high school and Tennessee's students do better on most of the achievement tests. But Georgia spends more dollars per student, and they have a lot more libraries.

Tome Test
Tennessee thinks the high-school graduation rate tells the most about the education systems because without a high school diploma, it's tough in the modern world!

State Facts
p.34
(Your states and statistics may be different.)

States: Indiana and Illinois

1. Capital
  IN – Indianapolis
  IL – Springfield

2. Tourist attractions (top 3)
  IN – Lincoln Log Cabin
  Historic Site, George Rogers
  Clark Park, Wyandotte Cave
  IL – Chicago museums and
  parks, Lincoln shrines at
  Springfield

3. Climate
  IN – 4 distinct seasons with a
  temperate climate
  IL – temperate; typically
  cold, snowy winters, hot
  summers

4. Tourism expenditures
  IN – $5.6 billion (1999)
  IL – $19.6 billion (1997)

5. Famous natives
  IN – Larry Bird, James
  Dean, Michael Jackson
  IL – Hillary Rodham
  Clinton, Ernest Hemingway,
  Jane Addams

Tome Test
I think New York would be the best one to visit because it spends the most on tourists, and she may be able to see Barbra Streisand buying a muffin on the street or something.

Populations
p.36

U.S. POPULATION FACTS AND STATISTICS (YEAR 2000 STATISTICS)

1. 281,421,906

2. 138,054,000

3. 4,239,587

4. 19,352,000

5. California / 33,871,648

6. Washington, DC* / 9,378 people per square mile

7. New York City / 8,008,278

8. Los Angeles County / 9,519,338

9. New York, NY / 81,417 in 1998

*Washington, DC isn't exactly a state, but it's listed as such in the census. The actual state with the highest population density is New Jersey, with 1,134.5 people per square mile.

Tome Test
Location
2.8 miles east of
Edgar Springs, MO
Latitude
37°41'49" N
Longitude
91°48'34" W

Nations of the World
p.38

(All data is from the most recent year for which information is provided. Your answer will vary depending on the year your almanac was published.)

1. Population
Costa Rica   3,773,057
Mauritius   1,189,825
Mozambique   19,371,057

2. Population density (per square mile)
Costa Rica   193
Mauritius   1,669
Mozambique   64

3. Government
Costa Rica   Republic
Mauritius   Republic
Mozambique   Republic

4. Chief crops (top 3)
Costa Rica
coffee, bananas, sugar
Mauritius
sugarcane, corn, potatoes
Mozambique
cashews, cotton, sugar

5. Number of TV sets (per 1,000 pop.)
Costa Rica   102
Mauritius   150
Mozambique   3.5

6. Daily newspaper circulation (per 1,000 pop.)
Costa Rica   102
Mauritius   49
Mozambique   8

7. Life expectancy
Costa Rica   Female 76.68
                Male   73.49
Mauritius   Female 75.31
                Male   67.26
Mozambique   Female 35.62
                Male   37.25

8. Fish catch (metric tons)

Costa Rica	33,613
Mauritius	13,852
Mozambique	39,579

9. Literacy

Costa Rica	95%
Mauritius	83%
Mozambique	40%

10. Tourism

Costa Rica	$1 billion
Mauritius	$545 million
Mozambique	NA

Tome Test
Country
Costa Rica

Fish catch per person
33,613 / 3,773,057 =
.009 metric tons each
(Fish catch divided
by population)

U.S. History
p.40
(These are just a few of the thousands of events your almanac lists in its U.S. history section.)

1807 Robert Fulton makes first steamboat trip.

1824 Pawtucket, RI, weavers strike is the first strike by women.

1833 Oberlin college is the first to offer coeducation.

1883 Brooklyn Bridge opens, the longest of its kind.

1903 First successful flight of an airplane.

1916 Jeanette Rankin is elected first ever female member of the House.

1948 President Truman defeats Thomas E. Dewey in major upset.

1962 James Meredith becomes the first black student at University of Mississippi.

Tome Test
Year: 1984
(Tennessee's birth year)

1. Astronauts aboard the *Challenger* were the first to fly free of a spacecraft.
2. Ronald Reagan beat Walter Mondale for the presidency in a landslide.

Sports
p.42
Year: 1976

NBA Champion: Boston
NBA Finals MVP: Jo Jo White

NFL Super Bowl Champion: Pittsburgh
Super Bowl MVP: Lynn Swann

NHL Stanley Cup Champion: Montreal
Stanley Cup MVP: Reg Leach

MLB World Series Champion: Cincinnati
World Series MVP: Johnny Bench

ROOKIES OF THE YEAR
Player
1972 NBA: Sidney Wicks
1998 NFL: Randy Moss
1982 NHL: Dale Hawerchuk
1977 MLB: Eddie Murray

(American League) and Andre Dawson (National League)

AWARD WINNERS
Player/s
1993 Cy Young Award Winners: Jack McDowell and Greg Maddux
(Major League Baseball)

1990 Art Ross Trophy Winner: Wayne Gretzky
(National Hockey League)

1998 John R. Wooden Award Winner: Antawn Jamison
(college basketball)

1989 Outland Award Winner: Mohammed Elewonibi
(college football)

1957 Vezina Trophy Winner: Jacques Plante
(National Hockey League)

Tome Test
Washington, DC

Awards and Prizes
p.44

AWARDS, MEDALS AND PRIZES
Nobel Prize: Literature 1936
Eugene O'Neill

Academy Award: Best Picture
1984
Amadeus

Caldecott Medal 1992
David Wiesner, *Tuesday*

Emmy Award: Comedy 1985
The Cosby Show

Grammy Award: Album of the
Year 1978
Bee Gees, *Saturday Night Fever*

Newberry Medal 1970
William H. Armstrong, *Sounder*

Miss America 1971
Phyllis Ann George

Nobel Prize: Physics 1950
Cecil F. Powell

Spingarn Medal 1991
Gen. Colin Powell

Pulitzer Prize: Fiction 1996
Richard Ford

Nobel Prize: Peace 1989
Dalai Lama

Tony Award: Musical 2001
The Producers

National Book Award: Fiction
1967
Bernard Malamud, *The Fixer*

Pulitzer Prize: Poetry 1982
Sylvia Plath

Tome Test
Caldecott Medal:
Children's book illustrator
Newberry Medal:
Children's book writer

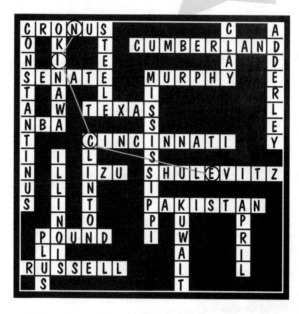

**MIA PHARAOH'S DANGEROUS
PUZZLE OF PAIN 1**
p.46

*Extra Dangerous
Password Question*

PASSWORD: Nice

Chamber 2
Dictionary

*(Using Merriam Webster's Collegiate
Dictionary: 10th Edition)*

Dictionary Abbreviations
p.50

1. adjective

2. stempceden

3. Middle French

4. No–it has a Latin derivation.

5. quakatootlesque

6. 1545

7. deleisonary
quakatootle
stumpsede

8. *pl* = plural

9. Late Latin

Tome Test

Part of Speech	adj.
Latin Form	affabilis
Noun Form	affability
Synonym	gracious

Syllables and Pronunciation
p.52

Dictionary	Phonetic
beau	'bō
clammy	'kla-mē
desperate	'des-p(ə)-rət
fake	'fāk
family	'fam-lē
hallelujah	ha-lə-'lü-yə
hungry	'hən-grē
love	'ləv
marriage	'mar-ij
marvelous	'märv-ə-ləs
muscle	'mə-səl
poignant	'pȯi-nyənt
shampoo	sham-'pü
virile	'vir-əl

1. Which words DO NOT have a stress on the first syllable?
hallelujah and shampoo

2. How does your dictionary represent the pronunciation of "-poo" in *shampoo*?
-'pü

3. How does your dictionary represent the pronunciation of "hun-" in hungry?
hən-

4. How many syllables are in the dictionary's pronunciation of the word *family*?
two or three
'fam-lē or 'fa-mə-lē

5. How does your dictionary represent the pronunciation of "cla-" in "clammy"?
'kla-

Tome Test

Name
1. Tennessee Toledo

Pronunciation
'te-nə-sē tə-'lē-(ˌ)dō
2. (your name here)

Parts of Speech
p.54

Words	#	Parts of Speech
life	2	n, adj
gain	2	n, vb
smile	2	vb, n
humor	2	n, vb
stir	2	vb, n
love	2	n, vb
stick	2	n, vb
treasure	2	n, vb
help	2	vb, n
answer	2	n, vb

Tome Test

Two   'liv and 'līv

Multiple Meanings
p.56

few
Dictionary definition as used in letter: *adj* at least some, but indeterminately small in number.

friend
Dictionary definition as used in letter: *n* one attached to another by affection or esteem, or *n* a favored companion.

deep
Dictionary definition as used in letter: *adv* to a great depth.

queen
Dictionary definition as used in letter: *n* a female monarch.

Prefixes
p.58

Prefix	Definition
a-	on; in; at
dis-	do the opposite of; not; deprive of
inter-	between; among; in the midst
mis-	badly, wrongly
post-	after; subsequent; later
pre-	earlier than; prior to; before
re-	again; back
semi-	half in quality or value
super-	over and above; higher in quantity, quality; more than
un-	do the opposite of; reverse

Prefix Word Examples

(Note: These are examples. Your words may be different.)

abed: in bed.

discomfort: physical unease (*not* comfort).

international: affecting two or more nations (*between* nations).

misconduct: improper (*bad*) behavior.

postclassical: relating to a period following (*after*) a classical one.

prerequisite: something that is necessary to an end (*before*

reaching that end).

refinish: to give furniture a new surface (to surface it *again*).

semiannual: occurring every six months (*half* a year).

superhuman: *exceeding normal* human power, size or capability.

unattractive: not pretty (the *opposite* of attractive).

Tome Test
Mia Pharaoh feels discomfort when she talks about explorer Rowdy Raines.

Suffixes
p.60

Word	Suffix forms
think	thinking, thinker
follow	follower, followed, following
feel	feelings
like	liked, liking, likable
remind	reminder, reminding
clever	cleverish, cleverness
use	used, using
do	doing, doable

Tome Test
Mia Pharaoh remembers liking Rowdy, but she never considered him much of a thinker.

Spelling Variations
p.62

Word / Alternate Spelling / Common Use

1. matzo / matzoh / equal
2. chili / chile / slightly more
3. descendant / descendent / equal
4. eurythmic / eurhythmic / slightly more
5. karoo / karroo / equal
6. license / licence / slightly more
7. pannier / panier / much more
8. sambar / sambur / equal
9. theater / theatre / equal
10. whizbang / whizzbang / much more

Tome Test
See your dictionary for the definitions of all of these words.

Word Origins
p.64

cake *n.*
Dictionary Etymology
[ME, fr. ON *kaka*; akin to OHG *kuocho* cake]

Translation
Cake comes from Middle English, which took the word from the Old Norse *kaka*, a word like the Old High German word *kuocho*, which means "cake."

candy *n.*
Dictionary Etymology
[ME *sugre candy*, part trans. of MF *sucre candi*, part trans. of OIt *zucchero candi*, fr. *zucchero* sugar + Ar *qandi* candied, fr. *qand* cane sugar]

Translation
Candy comes from the Middle English *sugre candy*, which is a partial translation of the Middle French, which is a partial translation of the Old Italian *zucchero candi*, which comes from *zucchero*, which means "sugar," and the Arabic *qandi*, which comes from *qand*, cane sugar.

chicken *n.*
Dictionary Etymology
[ME *chiken*, fr. OE *cicen* young chicken; akin to OE *cocc* cock]

Translation
Chicken comes from the Middle English word *chiken*, which comes from the Old English *cicen*, meaning "young chicken." *Cicen* is like the Old English *cocc*, meaning "cock."

fish *n.*
Dictionary Etymology
[ME, fr. OE *fisc*; akin to OHG *fisc* fish, L *piscis*]

Translation
Fish comes from Middle English, which got the word from the Old English word *fisc*. *Fisc* is related to the Old High German word *fisc*, meaning

"fish," and comes from the Latin *piscis*.

pasta *n.*
Dictionary Etymology
[It, fr. LL]

Translation
Pasta is an Italian word that comes directly from Late Latin.

Tome Test
cake (13c)
candy (15c)
chicken (14c)
fish (bef. 12c)
pasta (1874)

Latin Roots
p.66
Word / Root / Meaning
1. confuse / confusus / -na-
2. distraught / *distractus* / -na-
3. dour / *durus* / hard
4. elate / *elatus* / to carry out, elevate
5. excite / *excitare* / to rouse
6. incredulous / *incredulus* / -na-
7. love / *lubere* / *libere,* to please
8. morose / *morosus* / capricious
9. passion / *pati* / to suffer
10. sad / *satis* / enough

Tome Test
flustered
Scandinavian, *flaustur*

Mia Pharaoh's Dangerous Puzzle of Pain 2
p.68

1. heroine
2. anti-
3. four
4. noun, verb, adjective, adverb
5. hutzpa
6. *hutzpah* is used slightly more
7. science (biology)
8. first
9. *soror*
10. *systir*
11. synonymized, synonymizing
12. French
13. tomato

Extra Dangerous Password Question

PASSWORD:

Pharaohs

Chamber 3
World Atlas

(Using Rand McNally / Goode's World Atlas: 20th Edition)

Locating Maps
p.72
(Times will vary from reader to reader. The following answers are for which section would generally be the fastest place to look for a good map in your atlas.)

Place	Fastest Section
Africa	TOC
St. Louis	Index
Russia	Index
Atlantic Ocean	TOC
New Zealand	about the same
France	about the same
Bogota	Index
Okefenokee Swamp	Index
Somalia	Index
Aleppo	Index

Tome Test
Mogadishu:
Its type size is larger and its marker dot is bigger.

Map Symbols
p.74

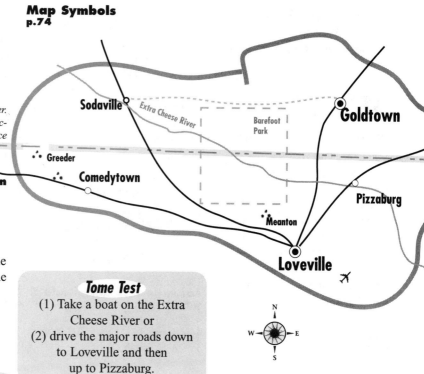

Tome Test
(1) Take a boat on the Extra Cheese River or
(2) drive the major roads down to Loveville and then up to Pizzaburg.

Directions
p.76

France
Furthest north?   Paris
Furthest east?   Lyon

Russia
Furthest south?   Moscow
Furthest east?   Moscow

South America
Furthest east?   Trinidad and Tobago
Furthest south?   Ecuador

Japan
Furthest west?   Osaka
Furthest north?   Yokohama

Europe
Furthest south?   Spain
Furthest east?   Poland

West Indies or Miami, Florida
Furthest north?   Miami
Furthest west?   Havana

South Korea
Furthest north?   Seoul
Furthest west?   Seoul

ANSWER PAGES

Tome Test
1. West Indies
2. Mexico and Caribbean Lands

Map Coordinates
p.78

Place	Coordinates
Asuncion, Paraguay	C6
Buenos Aries, Argentina	C7
Caracas, Venezuela	B1
Georgetown, Guyana	C1
Guayaquil, Ecuador	A3
La Paz, Bolivia	B4
Lima, Peru	A4
Paramaribo, Suriname	C1
Santiago, Chile	B7
Sao Paulo, Brazil	D5

Latitude and Longitude 1
p.80

Romantic Place	Latitude	Longitude
Amsterdam, Netherlands	52°21′N	4°52′E
Antananarivo, Madagascar	18°51′S	47°40′E
Barcelona, Spain	41°25′N	2°08′E
Casablanca, Morocco	33°32′N	7°41′W
Greenwich, England*	51°28′N	0°00′
Kingston, Jamaica	18°00′N	76°45′W
Melbourne, Australia	37°52′S	145°08′E
Moscow, Russia	55°45′N	37°37′E
Rio De Janeiro, Brazil	22°50′S	43°20′W
South Pole	90°00′S	0°00′

*Some atlases list Greenwich at 0°01′E

Tome Test
1. Greenwich and the South Pole
2. Moscow
3. Kingston

Latitude and Longitude 2
p.82

Lat./Long.: 31°19′N, 103°46′W
Place 1: Toyah, Texas

Lat./Long.: 10°35′S, 105°40′E
Place 2: Christmas Island

Lat./Long.: 19°45′N, 73°35′W
Place 3: Saint Nicolas Cape, Haiti

Lat./Long.: 90°00′N, 0°00′
Place 4: North Pole

Lat./Long.: 36°17′S, 148°30′E
Place 5: Snowy Mountains, Australia

Scale and Distance
p.84

Map: India
Scale: 1cm = 50 miles
Ratlam to Jamshedpur, India
11 cm = 550 miles

Map: China and Japan
Scale: 1cm = 100 miles
Shanghai, China to Hiroshima, Japan
7 cm = 700 miles

Map: Southern Japan
Scale: 1 cm = 40 kilometers
Kurume to Yawatahama, Japan
4.5 cm = 180 kilometers

Map: Asia
Scale: 1 cm = 400 kilometers
Moscow, Russia to Hovd, Mongolia
9 cm = 3,600 kilometers

Tome Test
Memphis to:

Gadsen, Alabama
3.5 cm = 262.5 miles

Pontiac, Michigan
9 cm = 675 miles

Boston, Massachusetts
15 cm = 1,125 miles

Elevation and Depth
p.86

Place: Mount Airy, North Carolina in the Blue Ridge Mountains
Elevation/Depth (in *feet*): 1,000-2,000 feet high

Place: The Atlantic Ocean, just off the coast of Charleston, South Carolina
Elevation/Depth (in *feet*): 0-500 feet deep

Place: The Atlantic Ocean
Elevation/Depth (in *meters*):
more than 6,100 meters deep

Place: Western Sahara
Elevation/Depth (in *meters*): 0-
152.5 meters high

Place: Algeria: Ahaggar Mountains
Elevation/Depth (in *feet*): 5,000-
10,000 feet high

Place: Chad, Tibesti Mountains
Elevations/Depth (in *meters*):
1,525-3,050 meters high

Tome Test
Tibesti: 11,204 feet
(Emi Koussi Mtn.)

Ahaggar: 9,541 feet
(Tahat Mtn.)

World Maps: Physical
p.88

1. Australia
   Africa
   South America

2. Asia
   Africa
   North America

3. Antarctica
   Europe

4. 10,000-20,000 feet

5. Any four of the following:
   Aegean
   Adriatic
   Baltic

Barents
Black
Caspian
Mediterranean
North
White

6. Indian Ocean

7. Pacific Ocean

8. Europe

9. Africa

10. North America
South America
Antarctica

World Maps: Political
p.90

1. South Africa
2. Peru
3. Mexico
4. Russia
5. Mediterranean
6. Pakistan
7. Yes
8. No
9. Japan
10. Nigeria
11. Ecuador
    Peru
    Colombia
    Brazil
12. Sea of Japan
13. Iceland

Tome Test
Africa

Six countries: Somalia, Kenya,
Uganda, Dem. Rep. of Congo,
Congo, Gabon.

Beyond the Maps 1
p.92

They're all true!

Beyond the Maps 2
p.94

POPULATION
1. False
2. True

LANGUAGES
3. False – They speak mostly
Romance and American Indian
languages.
4. True – And that's just a partial
list.

HEALTH AND LIFE EXPECTANCY
5. True
6. True

AGRICULTURE
7. True
8. False – A large central portion
is not farmed.

**ENERGY PRODUCTION AND
CONSUMPTION**
9. False
10. True

Tome Test
Iran

Mia Pharaoh's Dangerous Puzzle of Pain 3
p.96

Extra Dangerous Password Question

PASSWORD: Finish

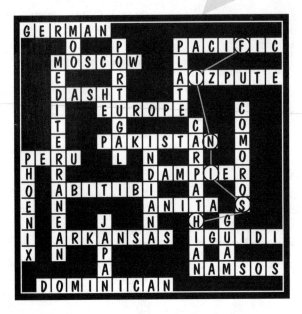

Chamber 4 Thesaurus
(Using Roget's International Thesaurus: 6th Edition)

Word Categories
p.100

(As long as you wrote down three categories for each of these word classes, you are right! Following are three examples from each word class. Check to make sure your words are in the same classes as these are.)

Chapter 1:
The Body and the Senses
Strength
Power
Femininity

Chapter 2: Feelings
Cheerfulness
Pride
Envy

Chapter 3:
Place and Change of Place
Leading
Ascent
Town, City

Chapter 4: Measure and Shape
Greatness
Superiority
Rarity

Chapter 5: Living Things
Youth
Life
Death

Chapter 6: Natural Phenomena
Season
Rain
Wind

Chapter 7: Behavior and the Will
Victory
Cunning
Attack

Chapter 8: Language
Meaning
Elegance
Eloquence

Chapter 9:
Human and Society Institutions
Divorce, Widowhood
Master
Aristocracy, Nobility, Gentry

Chapter 10: Values and Ideals
Right
Honor
Virtue

Chapter 11: Arts
Musician
Sculpture
Architecture, Design

Tome Test
# of Categories: 1075
First Category: Birth
Last Category: Space Travel

Using the Index
p.102
(Your synonym choices may be different.)

beautiful
1. artistic — 712.20
2. beauteous — 1016.18

intelligent
1. teachable — 570.18
2.. mental — 919.7

strong
1. forceful — 15.15
2. energetic — 17.13

faithful
1. person of honor — 644.8
2. zealous — 101.9

independent
1. free agent — 430.12
2. neutral — 467.4

money
1. wealth — 618.1
2. currency — 728.1

power
1. strength — 15.1
2. energy — 17.1

Finding Synonyms 1
p.104

Word	Best Synonym
1.	
permit	let
perspire	sweat

New Rule: Never <u>let</u> them see you <u>sweat</u>.

2.	
crayon	pen
saber	sword

New Rule: The <u>pen</u> is mightier than the <u>sword</u>.

3.	
conveyance	wagon
equine	horse

Don't put the <u>wagon</u> in front of the <u>horse</u>.

4.	
busted	broken
repair	fix

New Rule: If it's not <u>broken</u>, don't <u>fix</u> it.

5.	
intimates	friends
kinfolk	family

New Rule: <u>Friends</u> may come and go, but <u>family</u> is forever.

6.	
chortles	laughs
guffaws	laughs

New Rule: He who <u>laughs</u> last <u>laughs</u> longest.

7.	
separate	divide
vanquish	conquer

New Rule: <u>Divide</u> and <u>conquer</u>!

Tome Test
false alarm = flash in the pan
consent = okay

Finding Synonyms 2
p.106

LITTLE WOODROW

Word	Opposite	Synonym
tired	excited	exhilarated
weird	normal	natural
always	never	at no time
sick	healthy	in fine fettle
divorce	marry	get hitched

My first husband was Little Woodrow. At first, his jokes made me laugh. After a while, they made me <u>exhilarated</u>. He talked with a <u>natural</u> accent, he was <u>at no time</u> worrying, he was always <u>in fine fettle</u>, and he couldn't keep his eyes off other women. Once, I found him kissing my best friend Cleopatra! That's when I knew I had to <u>get hitched</u> to him. Lucky for him, he died first.

BIG PHRANK

Word	Opposite	Synonym
ugly	attractive	alluring
thin	thick	dense
huge	small	minute
terrible	wonderful	extraordinary
over	starting	taking off

My second husband was Big Phrank. He was much older than I was, and very <u>alluring</u>. His hair was <u>dense</u>, his belly was <u>minute</u>, and his choice in clothes was <u>extraordinary</u>. So why did I marry him? He was rich and famous. He had been a great entertainer in his youth. His nickname was Chairman of the Gourd because he played the gourd-flute like a dream. When I married him, his career was really <u>taking off</u>.

Tome Test

attraction	repulsion
together	apart
close	far

Mia Pharaoh's Dangerous Puzzle of Pain 4
p.108

CHAPTER 16:
WHY I SHOULD RULE THE WORLD

1. contemporary
2. relevant
3. chance
4. call the shots
5. bossy
6. foes
7. conquering
8. kitty-cats
9. make a deal
10. tome

Extra Dangerous Password Question

PASSWORD: Last

Extra Dangerous Password that Releases Tennessee!

NICE
PHARAOHS
FINISH
LAST

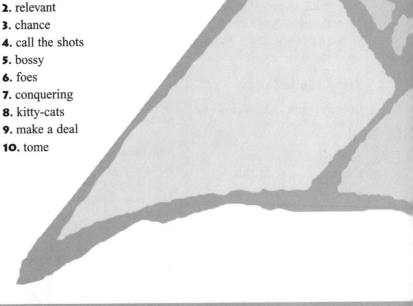

CONGRATULATIONS!